BOOMER SELLING^{SM}

**helping the
wealthiest generation
in history
own your
premium products
and services**

STEVE HOWARD

ACTION:PRESS
Increased Profits Through Knowledge™

Phoenix, Arizona

Copyright © 2009 by Steve Howard

Published by ACTion Press, Phoenix Arizona

First Edition

International Standard Book Number 978-0-9821911-0-1

Library of Congress Control Number: 2008942222

Request for permissions should be addressed to:
The ACT Group, Inc.
201 West Orchid Lane
Phoenix, Arizona 85021
(800) 515 0034

Printed in the United States of America.

www.BoomerSelling.com

For my grandchildren
Liam, Abbey, Kai and Miles

TABLE OF CONTENTS

Crack the Boomer Code

Boomer Selling was written to help you increase your income in any economy by helping the wealthiest generation in history acquire the premium products and services we're dying to have. We (I'm a Boomer) control over 50% of discretionary spending and 70% of the wealth in the U.S., more than $33 trillion by a recent estimate. We're well worth the trouble, especially now. Even when economic times become grim and people lose their jobs, we're more likely to have money saved, home equity to tap, executive jobs that aren't going anywhere. If we want it enough, most Boomers can find the money to buy the premium products you're selling.

The Voice of Your Customer

Let me ask you this: How much would you pay to sit in a room with your best, most influential customers for an entire day and have them tell you exactly what you need to do to get them to willingly buy your premium products and services? Better yet, three of these clients will share their special insights into today's Boomer buyers. They include:

- A psychologist, who will provide an entertaining insight into what drives Boomer buying behavior.

- A sociologist, who will provide a sometimes irreverent look at Boomer culture and explain our rapidly changing need to consume greater quantities of premium products and services.

- A very successful sales consultant who will reveal the extremely powerful common-sense sales process he uses to create delighted Boomer buyers, and a full appointment calendar of pre-sold referrals.

Some of the things you are going to learn about Baby Boomers include:

- What turns us on

- What ticks us off

- What to do and not do in order to get Boomers to trust you

- How to ethically and systematically eliminate all competition
- How to consistently sell premium (high margin) solutions
- How to eliminate most objections before they're raised
- How to create an endless flow of pre-sold referrals, and much more

Business and industry spends billions of dollars every year to learn about their customers. What are they thinking? What are their greatest needs? How would they prefer to buy? Everyone wants to unlock the minds of the richest generation in history. With this book, you're going to get that information straight and unvarnished from Boomer buyers. You're going to get the secrets to cracking the Boomer code. Is that worth your time?

About the author

I am the average Baby Boomer, the person in the middle of the Baby Boomer belief bell curve. I've been to Haight Ashbury once and Vietnam twice. I've owned a Mustang, a VW bug and a Ford Pinto. I've seen George Jones, The Grateful Dead and the birth and death of disco. The 1970's recession taught me how to find hidden opportunities in tough times. The '80s savings and loan crisis turned out to be a great time to start a company to help business owners and sales consultants, *"Increase Profits Through Knowledge.™"* The early '90s recession provided the perfect opportunity to show our clients how to increase profits and eliminate competition by selling high-margin, premium products and services. I'm anxious to help you grow sales and profits in this new era of apprehension and amazing opportunity.

Hand Me That Eight Track Tape

Selling to Boomers is more than learning steps in a process; you've got to get to know what makes us tick. This is especially true for non-Boomers. I know there is a good chance that you're part of Generation X (1965-1982) or Generation Y (1982-2004), so some of the cultural and historical references throughout *Boomer Selling* may be new to you. This is deliberate, and there are two reasons for it:

- First, to help you understand some of the important (and sometimes silly) things Boomers use as our frame of reference. The more you understand our personal touchstones and appreciate how we feel about the things we remember and care about, the faster our defenses drop, the more we trust you, and the easier it is for us to share our wildest hopes and deepest desires.

- Second, every unfamiliar example or anecdote reveals how many opportunities there are to get to know us better. The more you understand us the easier it is for you to match the way you sell to the way we prefer to buy.

"Change isn't necessary because survival isn't mandatory."
– W. Edwards Deming

You might be asking yourself, "Why should I change what I'm doing now? Do I really need to know how to sell to Baby Boomers?" That depends on where you want to go in the future. Every economic crisis creates a crossroads. The unmarked road leads to fear, frustration and possible failure. The marked road, the one that leads to sales success and financial freedom has a signpost ... it reads: *Boomer Selling*.

Future Profits Require Boomer Buyers

After escaping from Sing-Sing prison and being on the lam for over 18 years, notorious bank robber Willy Sutton was arrested in Sunnyside, NY in 1950. After his first court appearance a local reporter asked, "Mr. Sutton, why do you rob banks?" Without hesitation Sutton gave what has become a classic answer to a no-brainer question: "That's where the money is." Though he couldn't have known it, Sutton also answered the question you probably had when you picked up this book and asked yourself, "Why should I learn how to sell to Baby Boomers?" Because, friend, that's where the money is!

77 million Baby Boomers were raised in a time of unbelievable opportunity and unlimited prosperity by parents who struggled to survive the Great Depression and World War II. That experience, being reared by peo-

ple who had been steeped in self-sacrifice and making do with less—even as we were experiencing television, boat-like Chrysler automobiles and endless possibilities—colored our entire lives and had a tremendous influence on what we buy, how we buy it and who we'll buy it from.

Baby Boomers are, hands down, the most complicated people you'll ever work with in a sales situation. A look under the Boomer hood reveals some fascinating and often confounding realities about us:

- We're smart and insecure, caring and direct, confident and suspicious.

- We've seen every sales trick and hate most of them. We were the vanguard of consumer culture, so marketers and sales people have been trying to sell to us since we saw our first breakfast cereal commercial on a 12" black and white TV. Sales tricks and pressure tactics do nothing but insult us.

- Thanks to our parents, we know the value of every penny. We might buy a $1,000 suit at Nordstrom, then stop at Wal-Mart for socks.

- Sometimes we're irrational. More than one Boomer has remodeled their kitchen with a monstrous six-burner stainless steel range then never use it for more than heating water for hot chocolate.

- We'll bargain at the drop of a hat. We love squeezing concessions from sales consultants and our favorite question is, "Is that the best you can do?"

- We consider ourselves special. We're sure that we're unlike anyone who has ever come along in human history and we feel that we deserve to be recognized for our uniqueness...every single one of us.

So, if Boomers are such tough customers and hard bargainers, why bother with us? Why invest your valuable time learning the best way to sell to us? Because we are where the money is! We may be wary and savvy and impatient and maybe a little egotistical at times, but we're also loyal and love to give referrals to people who go out of their way to take care of us. We're a lot of work and you have to know how to work with us the right way, but if you can earn our trust and confidence, we'll be the best customers you ever had.

We can make you rich

Boomers may not have one foot in the grave and the other foot on a banana peel, but we know there's a Chiquita plantation around the corner. We've started realizing that if we don't spend the money we've got locked up in home equity, saving accounts and investments pretty soon, the government will be glad to spend it for us. Once we come face-to-face with the scary fact that we have more days behind us than ahead of us, our lives and lifestyles move into a new and exciting phase. Old wants are replaced with new wants. We want to build memories in everything we do. We want to build a tangible legacy to pass on to our children and grandchildren. We want to take that cruise or build the cabin we've always dreamed of. We want to buy products and services that make our life better in a meaningful way. We want to change the world, or at least make it more beautiful.

Our awareness of mortality has helped us realize three things about buying cheap stuff.

1. We may be slow learners, but we finally figured out how a lot of companies can sell their products so cheap: they make their money fixing them.

2. In the past, we all bought the cheap stuff, and then ended up buying something better after it quit working. We've bought the least expensive hedge trimmers only to have the handles break the first time we used them. We've hired the discount contractor to build a room addition only to kick ourselves after having to fire them for incompetence and hire someone to redo all their work at twice the price. No more!

3. We've learned we will never get more than we pay for. We've figured out that the cheapest products can end up being the most expensive, and we're not interested.

Old-School Sales Tactics Make Us Mad

Boomers can be your greatest source of high margin sales and pre-sold referrals or we can be your worst nightmare. It all depends on the type of sales process you use. When we were growing up we saw one too many unscrupulous used car salesmen and door-to-door scam artists pressure and bamboozle our parents into buying something they didn't want and couldn't afford. We even put up with that abuse for a while, but not any longer. We've seen the strategies and pressure moves too many times, and we despise them.

Most Boomers' feelings about traditional sales methods can be compared to the famous scene in the movie *Network*, where Howard Beale, played by Peter Finch, tells his TV news audience to stick their heads out the window and scream "I'm as mad as hell and I'm not going to take this anymore!" Before long, the entire city of New York is shouting.

> **If you want to do business with us, you've got to sell the way we want to buy**

"I'm as mad as hell and I'm not going to take this anymore!"

That's how we feel. We're tired of old-school sales tricks, canned questions and worn-out sales phrases. Boomers have always wanted to change the world by changing the rules, and the way we see it, it's time we started playing the sales game by our rules, not yours. If you try to strong-arm or manipulate us, we'll raise enough objections to make your head explode, or we'll just walk out without another word.

We're sick of false sincerity, phony flattery and limited-choice sales approaches. Turn-of-the-nineteenth-century sales tactics like "good-better-best" turn us off. When we're asked to chose from three package deals, we start getting this queasy feeling in the pit of our stomachs as we realize one of two things is going to happen: We won't get exactly what we want. Or, we'll end up paying for something "included in the package" that we don't want.

Please don't limit us to three choices! Give us unlimited choices. Be a consultant, not a sales robot! If we're spending a lot of money, let us customize what we're buying around our requirements, not yours. Get to know us; communicate with us and find out what needs we're trying to satisfy. The more you understand Boomers, the more you know for sure; "that's where the money is."

We'd rather accumulate wealth than show it

Too many poor sales consultants have fallen on their faces trying to guess how much money we have based on the houses we live in, the clothes we wear or the cars we drive. That's a sucker's game. Don't do it, unless you want to live paycheck to paycheck. It's easy to underestimate our ability to buy the best, because a lot of us like to keep our financial resources well hidden (a lot of us also feel guilty we have so much more than our struggling parents did, even though that's exactly what they would have wanted). Many of us live in unassuming neighborhoods, drive older vehicles, cut our own lawns, wear Timex watches and buy clothes off the rack when they go on sale. As Thomas J. Stanley and William D. Danko wrote in their bestselling book *The Millionaire Next Door*, most wealthy Americans live ordinary-looking lives. But when we really want something, we'll pay full price and be darned glad we did. See what I mean by complex?

So, if you can't determine what we want to spend based on our appearance how are you supposed to know what you can sell us? The Boomer Selling process is all about getting past surface assumptions and learning ways to connect with Boomers and find out what we desire, what we fear, and what our motivations for buying really are. The Boomer Selling process is your ticket to turning us into your best customers.

The Boomer Selling Process

Three things must be in place before Boomers will buy from you:

1. We must want what you're selling

2. The perceived value of what you're offering must exceed its price

3. We must be able to afford it

If you're selling the best, most Boomers want it. We grew up with plenty, then suffered through the economic downturn of the 1970s and '80s. We're not about to deprive ourselves again. We want premium products and solutions and aren't afraid to pay for them. Second, we're smart enough to know value when we see it. We understand the importance of reliability, quality materials, craftsmanship and topnotch service. Finally, we're the ones with the cash to spend. Baby Boomers can afford to buy more of what you're selling than all other demographic groups combined.

> **Baby Boomers can afford to buy more premium products than all other demographic groups combined**

We are the kings and queens of discretionary income.

Discretionary income is what allows Boomer buyers to move from bottom-tier goods to high-margin solutions. Our discretionary income is your ticket to big increases in sales, commissions and personal income. Our rising tide can lift your personal boat—*if* you know how to work with us. The way to do it is by using the straightforward common-sense Boomer Selling process:

- Step One: ***Create* Confidence**. Get us to trust you and believe that you have the knowledge and skill to help us get the perfect solution.

- Step Two: ***Determine* Desires**. Find out what desires (such as security or social standing) are driving our decision to shop in the first place, then find ways to satisfy our desires.

- Step Three: ***Customize* Solutions**. Boomers don't want the same product or solution as everyone else. Design a package of products, services and extras to come as close as possible to solving each particular problem.

- Step Four: ***Reduce* Risk**. Use the right information and Boomer friendly tools to reduce our risks both real and imagined.

- Step Five: ***Elevate* Emotions**. Create excitement and provide us with the emotional stimulation we need to buy the things we desire.

- Step Six: *Validate* **Value**. Educate your Boomer customers in the many ways your solution creates value and ensures that the value you're offering exceeds the price.

- Step Seven: *Attain* **Agreement**. If we haven't purchased by now, review the benefits and let us sell ourselves.

We're Premium Buyers Who Like to Spend

Why do you have to follow these seven interwoven steps? Because Boomers like to spend money, but we won't give it to just anyone. It's a self-preservation thing, but it's also a self-esteem thing. We like to take care of ourselves and to show our peers that we've made it, but we also want to know that we've invested well in things that are of value. We love feeling that we're wise, savvy shoppers who drive a hard bargain.

We're worth the time and self-education because we're your premium buyers. We don't do cheap unless the purchase has no meaning or we have no choice—especially since millions of Boomers are still working and not on fixed retirement incomes. This all means one thing for you: we're your best premium customers. We're the folks buying the 60" plasma televisions when other shoppers are settling for 48," and the $25,000 outdoor kitchens for our decks when younger families are just springing for a

Weber gas grill and a few deck chairs. We have most of the money, and we're not afraid to use it.

"That's where the money is..."

Some facts you'll want to know about us:

- Many Boomers are or will soon be empty nesters. After years of raising a family and paying for college, we'll finally have more money to spend on the things we want to buy. That means spas and garden tractors, bigger beds and better windows and gourmet kitchens.

- Unlike younger generations, who are lucky to have an employer match their 401k contribution, a large number of Boomers have built up substantial net worth in employer-sponsored, defined benefit retirement plans. So even when we're retired, we're going to have cash to spread around.

- The more years we live, the longer the magic of compound interest increases the value of our retirement accounts, CDs and the cash value of our life insurance.

- Many of us own our homes free and clear, or have built up tremendous home equity that we can tap if we want to buy something badly enough. And we do.

- When you count investment properties, vacation homes and primary residences, Boomers own half the homes in the U.S., many with gobs of untapped equity.

- We're the most likely generation to receive all of the money we've paid into Social Security Insurance since we got our first job bussing tables at 14.

- Many of us have the training and time to make serious money in the stock market, regardless of whether the Bulls or Bears are in charge.

- 50% of us have achieved some level of higher education, which fuels even higher incomes.

- A significant number of us started our own business, entered a profession like medicine or law, or became well paid sales consultants. So our earning power is unmatched.

- We know we're in our peak earning years and so we're maximizing every opportunity to acquire the things we want, now!

- A large number of us will continue working longer than any previous generation. AARP estimates that more than 60% of Boomers will continue to work in some way after leaving full-time employment.

- Our higher credit scores lower the cost to finance the big ticket items you sell.

- As our parents pass on, we will inherit what they didn't spend, almost $10 trillion, which, as the finance gurus say, is real money. We will invest some of that money, but we'll be looking to spend the rest, and a million companies, marketers and sales consultants will be working 24/7 to liberate some of those greenbacks from our wallets and purses.

ONE

Confidence is the foundation of all Boomer buying.

Create Confidence

The modern era of high pressure sales reached its stride just as the first Baby Boomers were being conceived. In the months following the end of World War II, hundreds of thousands of GIs returned home with their pockets bulging with money and their minds set on buying the ultimate symbol of freedom: a brand new automobile. Because the demand for new cars far outstripped the meager supply, automobile dealerships hired salesmen (in those day it was all men) to do two things:

- Qualify and weed out those who didn't have the ability to buy today
- Coerce, pressure and manipulate the folks who did have the money, to part with as much of it as was legally possible

With the exception of a few car dealerships, little has changed in over 60 years. By the time the leading edge

3

of the Baby Boomers reached middle age, we had met more than our fair share of greedy-to-the-bone, promise-anything rip-off artists whose only interest was cashing their next commission check. These walking stereotypes gave us such immortal (and incredibly annoying) phrases as, "I have to talk to my sales manager," "I can only offer you this price today," and "What do I have to do to sell you this car?" Think Joe Isuzu with less charm and a bad sport jacket and you've got the picture.

We also met just enough caring individuals, people who really seemed to listen and went out of their way to help us solve problems without sleazy, high-pressure sales tactics, that we didn't totally lose our faith in salespeople. Together, these years of positive experiences and infuriating, expensive lessons have come to shape every buying decision Boomers make today, especially when we're looking at something complex or unfamiliar like a bathroom remodel, financial planning, a high-tech security system, or home solar power plant.

We've been around the block enough to know when someone sees us as a wallet with legs, and when that happens we're not shy about taking our business to the dozens of competitors dying to get it. Sales professionals who aspire to become trusted long-term resources for their Boomer customers must live and breathe the following vital drivers of Boomer buying behavior.

The Handy-Dandy Rip-Off Prevention System

Imagine an old-fashioned traveling salesman, like Harold Hill straight out of *The Music Man*, pitching his audience on a dusty street:

> *"I'll tell you folks, there are salespeople out there who would love to get you to buy cars and condominiums and life insurance and televisions as big as your house, and you know what many of those snakes are going to tell you? Lies! That's right, lies! Believe it or not, ladies and gentlemen, some salespeople will lie through their crooked teeth to get your John Hancock on the bottom line. I hate to disillusion these beautiful children standing here—not so close son, you'll get fingerprints on the suit—but that's the way the world is. But what if I told you that there was a tool you could use to keep yourself from being ripped off by unscrupulous flim-flammers of all types? Yes, there is such a miracle, and it's called…The Rip-off Prevention System!"*

If we didn't already have a "Rip-Off Prevention System", even Boomers would buy one from this blowhard huckster. Why? Baby Boomers need the level of protection that our "Rip-Off Prevention System" provides. We have developed a powerful warning system born from years of being burned by unpleasant or dishonest sales hacks, and it's kept us from being taken advantage of again and again. Other people have "sales resistance." We have a "sales force field." We *hate* repeating past buying mistakes.

Too many sincere consultants lose sales because they don't understand how the Boomer "Rip-Off Prevention System" works. We file away the details of each inflated promise, disingenuous misrepresentation and lie in our subconscious minds. Forget about the positive sales experiences; those don't have the sticking power of the time we bought a vacuum that fell apart in 48 hours, or financed a car with the dealer only to spend two hours being interrogated like a hostile witness on the stand by someone trying to sell us a $500 road salt protection package.

Negative experiences have far more cognitive staying power than the positive.

So the moment we meet you, an unconscious evaluation system springs into action to protect us from being taken advantage of or repeating past mistakes. Within two seconds of shaking your hand, our brains will evaluate up to a dozen non-verbal clues from your attire and posture to your speech patterns and your choice of words. Our subconscious mind picks out a rogue's gallery of characteristics, and then scans our memory's hard drive trying to match elements from past good and bad sales experiences to what's happening now. When a connection is found, an electrical circuit running to our emotional response center snaps closed.

This snap-judgment process (think Malcolm Gladwell's bestseller *Blink*) is so powerful that expanding the conclusions we form about you, based on our two-second impression by 50% can take up to another four minutes. In other words, you've got two seconds to make us feel comfortable, or you're at best fighting an uphill battle to gain our confidence. A positive response to these subtle cues can create a sense of well-being. A negative signal can stir feelings of fear or apprehension. So it's vital to know the thinking that sets our Rip-off Prevention System in motion.

Rip-Off = "A bad deal"

The 18th century economist Adam Smith said, "The sole purpose of production is consumption." Boomers have done everything in our power to prove him right. We're the first generation of mega-consumers, brought up to believe in the boundless promise of advertising, nuclear energy, and science, science, science. When we were growing up, doctors were even telling us that smoking was healthy! Consequently, by the time we reached middle age, most Boomers have purchased more products and services than our parents and grandparents combined. We *are* the Consumer Culture. As a result, we know valid information and garbage when we hear them.

— Boomer Selling Insight —
The more things we buy, the greater
our chances of getting ripped-off

If that seems a little negative, it's a negativity that comes from a lifetime of hard lessons. Every Baby Boomer's "Rip-Off-Prevention System" gets a little harder to penetrate every time a salesperson says or does something that creates a negative emotional response due to its connection to a bad buying experience from the past. Anytime a salesperson attempts to breakdown these defenses with phony flattery, verbal manipulation, or subtle pressure, our self-protection system goes into high alert. We start getting defensive, find it hard to listen and may even start disliking the sales consultant.

On the other hand, every time our subconscious filing system finds a positive match, our guard drops a little, we listen harder, and we start liking and even trusting you. Each positive response increases our confidence that you are not just out to earn a commission but to really take care of us. As our confidence goes up, our stress level goes down, anxiety starts disappearing and apprehension is slowly replaced by a feeling of well-being.

The Combination to Door Number One is Trust

The first step in Boomer Selling is understanding how to disarm, unlock and turn off our "Rip-Off Prevention System." Imagine an old-fashioned two-door safe with a big round dial on one side with just 10 numbers on it. Each number is one "element of confidence." When enough of the numbers are dialed correctly, the first safe door opens revealing a stack of cash *and* another dial that will unlock a second door.

The most important thing Boomers shop for are people we can trust. Trust is absolute confidence in the honesty and reliability of another person. Unfortunately, Boomers have a natural unwillingness to place our confidence in sales consultants because we've met so many shifty sales people and been hit with so many shady sales tactics over the years. If we don't have confidence in you, we can't buy from you, it's just that simple.

The entire sale hinges on your ability to create confidence. Each of the following elements of confidence disengages one part of the first door's big lock. The more elements of confidence, the more likely you are to find the treasure hidden behind Door Number One. The elements:

1. Non-Verbal Clues

> *"Sometimes you can observe a lot by watching."*
> — *Yogi Berra*

Boomers tend to make buying decisions based on impressions and "gut feelings" (years of distilled good and bad buying experiences) more than features and facts.

We do this by looking for non-verbal clues that tell us that you as the sales consultant can be trusted. Before you open your mouth or reach out your hand, our subconscious mind is processing years of embedded experience to determine if you can be trusted. Make sure the first "clues" we see—posture, dress, grooming—shout "Trust!"

2. Enthusiasm

"Nothing great was ever achieved without enthusiasm."
– Ralph Waldo Emerson

Boomers love dealing with consultants who believe in what they're selling and share what they believe. Your level of enthusiasm helps determine how your message is received and believed. High, sincere enthusiasm is your greatest ally. In today's world of hype, noise and the non-stop bombardment of advertising you must show you're sold on what you're selling.

3. Likability

"The main work of a trial attorney
is to make a jury like his client."
– Clarence Darrow

It's virtually impossible to trust people we don't like. Think about the last time you met someone and it was like being with an old friend. Chances are this person had a firm handshake, warm smile and gave you three to seven seconds of repeated eye contact while you were talking. Sincere eye contact can be the shortest path to likability and trust. Why is eye contact so important? Because human eyes are the only part of the central nervous system that are in direct contact with another human being. Maybe that's why the Greeks called our eyes "the windows of the soul."

4. Sincere Interest

"Listening, not imitation, is the sincerest form of flattery."
— Dr. Joyce Brothers

We all share common interests with everyone we meet. The more meaningful these interests, the stronger the potential bond. Three interests people have in common and are usually anxious to talk about are their jobs, their family and recreational activities. We trust people who take time to learn about us. Dale Carnegie said, "You can make more friends in two months by becoming interested in other people than you can in two years by trying to get other people interested in you." One of the biggest reasons sales are lost is that the consultant simply didn't show enough interest in the buyer.

5. Listening

"I've never met a man who listened himself out of a job."

– Senator Evert Dirkson

The Japanese symbol for "listen" is formed from the character for "ear", surrounded by the character for "gate." When you listen to us, we allow you to enter the gate of our mind

Listening creates a bond of trust. We tend to like people who listen to us. We tend to agree with people we like. We buy from those we like and agree with.

6. Caring

Caring is measured by actions, not words. Talk is cheap. A Carnegie Foundation study found that while only 15% of business success is attributed to job knowledge and technical skills, 85% of success came from the ability to deal with people. Boomers go out of our way to give our business to consultants who care about us, our loved ones, and our well-being. We're desperate to find consultants who not only give us what we want but care enough to discover what we desire.

7. Discovering Problems

"What you do speaks so loudly I cannot hear what you say."

— Emerson

Boomers buy because we feel that the consultant understands our problems and concerns, not because we were made to understand the consultant's product or services. A lot of consultants talk a good game, but if you don't take the time to obtain the right information that allows you to solve our problems, we're not buying. Asking the right questions not only gives you the information you need, it also allows you to discover problems that were overlooked by your competition and set yourself apart from everyone else by being the one to meet needs we didn't even know we had.

8. Believability

In a court of law, the side with the
most compelling evidence usually wins.

The quickest way to lose trust is to say something that Boomer buyers don't believe. The catch: what you say can be 100% true, but we may not believe it. When that happens, you'd better have the evidence, documentation and data to back up your claims. If there are any potential problems or disadvantages, mention them, it flatters our intelligence and makes everything you say more believable.

9. Transparency

We don't trust people who hide things from us.

Are you doing anything we can't see or be part of? If so, bring us on board and make us part of the process. If you're adding numbers together, show us what you're doing. If you need to talk to someone else, let us meet them. Transparency lets us know you're not secretly trying to manipulate us or adding hidden costs or "traps" behind the scenes. If you play your cards too close to the vest like James Garner in *Maverick*, we're likely to think you're looking for a way to cheat us. Never underestimate the wariness of Boomer consumers.

10. Keep It Simple

Impress with your ability to make complex things simple.

One key to instilling confidence is keeping it simple (unless we have a Ph.D. from MIT, in which case we will want all the engineering specs). Break down the jargon and technical details to a point that we can easily understand then ask, "Would you like to know more?" This illustrates that you know what you're talking about without trying to impress us with techno-babble.

What's Behind Door Number Two?

Door Number Two requires more skill to unlock but it's well worth the extra effort. The prize hidden inside is your ticket to financial freedom. The most direct path to financial freedom is (appropriate fanfare and drum roll, please):

Selling premium products

A premium product is any good or service that provides more benefits and higher margins than the lowest-cost, minimum solution. Over 80% of all Boomers will pay more money to receive greater benefits. Once Boomers start buying premium products, our natural tendency is to quickly move up the scale towards the "best of the best."

Ask a Boomer what we associate with the word "salesperson" and chances are they'll say something like, "The sound of fingernails on a blackboard." We don't need a salesperson to sell us premium products. We know what we want. What we really need is a consultant to guide us through the maze of claims, hype and alternatives. When you take a consultative approach with Boomers, you become the product as much as the product itself or the company that makes it. In our view you're more important than any badge or logo. Your service and knowledge is what elevates your solution from being a commodity to being something of unique value.

— Boomer Selling Insight —
If we have confidence in you, up to 85% of
the time we'll go with the brand you recommend

Boomers hate dealing with untrained sales reps who don't know the products they're selling; we will gladly spend time with a trained expert who really knows his or her stuff. We want you to give us insider information. We want to feel like we will become more knowledge-able as a result of being educated by you. This turns us into smarter consumers and more knowledgeable buyers, which also helps you, because you don't have to "train" us in the future. The right information can form, reinforce or change our beliefs, and we won't buy until we believe.

It gets better. The more we learn from you, the more referrals you will get. We enjoy appearing smart to our friends by quoting the information you provide. We want you to have expert-level knowledge available at your fingertips so we can show you off to the people in our lives. That means more Boomer business for you. For example, let's say your prospects are in the market for carpeting for their entire home. Odds are they've bought carpeting many times before and don't need to hear the obvious from you. But they probably don't know about the stain repellent properties of the fibers or the best type of vacuum and vacuum setting to use for their regular cleaning—and if they have young grandkids who spend a lot of time on the floor, they'll care about those facts. If you're going to target Boomers in your sales, have the esoteric facts at hand, ready to present. When you do, you make an impression as an expert who knows the inside information and can help us get the perfect solution.

"Be a Specialist."

We've found it a lot less painful to deal with consultants who know what they are doing. In fact, a huge part of the solution we're buying is your expertise! We don't have the time or desire to become experts on buying what you sell. We want to find an expert we can trust instead of trying to evaluate other "experts." However, without your help, we don't know how to evaluate your expertise, so it's vital that you share what you know in a context we can understand.

Boomers know that specialists justify their higher price by doing the job right and giving their customers confidence that they will get 100% of the benefits and value they're paying for. We've learned that about 95 percent of the time if we don't deal with specialists on a complex purchase, something important will be overlooked and we could end up stuck with something that doesn't meet our needs and makes us regret ever setting foot in your store. Help us realize the multiple ways we might suffer if we make a mistake in selecting a product or service; explain to us in detail the risks and the rewards in working with you. Let us know that you, as a specialist, are here to help us avoid such mistakes.

Once you gain our full trust, everything you say will be an implied promise, a covenant that exists in our minds that says, "When I call John to help me with A, I will receive X, Y and Z every time." Once that promise is in place, it's your job to back it up *every single time.* If you fall short just once, you can torpedo the trust you've worked so hard to create. Trust is hard-built and easily shattered for us Boomers. Bottom line: we desperately need someone who is less interested in getting our money and more interested in establishing a trusting relationship, helping us solve problems, and finding ways to make our lives more physically and emotionally satisfying…someone who will focus on our self interest, not theirs. Sounds like a personal ad, but we don't like you in *that* way. We do want to give you the chance to get rich taking care of us. Here's how:

"Focus on me."

"The deepest need in nature is the craving to be appreciated."
– William James

Baby Boomers have been called self-centered, self-indulgent and self-absorbed. Many say we're only concerned with self-image, self-fulfillment and our own self-interest. Yeah, and…? First of all, who isn't concerned primarily with his or her own self-interest?

"When dealing with people, remember you are not dealing with creatures of logic, but with creatures of emotion, creators motivated by pride and vanity."

— *Dale Carnegie*

Even when we shop to buy a gift for someone else, every one of us is also interested in a gift that says something good about us. We're all so vain, we probably think this song is about us.

Mary Kay Ash cut to the chase when she advised, "Imagine everyone you meet is wearing a sign that says 'Make me feel important.'" The focus of every Boomer sale must be on the people buying, not the product you're selling. How can you solve problems? How can you make life easier? How can you create value?

"Monopolize listening."

"Some people without brains sure do a lot of talking."

— *The Wizard of Oz*

It's been recorded that Samson killed 3,000 Philistines with the jawbone of an ass. This same tool kills millions of sales every day. Probably the most common negative experience that Boomers tell me about is consultants who won't shut up and let them talk. That's just a bad strategy if you really want us to buy from you. You see, we know we're a unique generation that has shaped global culture. As a rule, we have very high self-esteem. Basically, we're pretty darned fascinating and we want you to know it.

We also know that it's impossible for consultants to learn anything about us when they're talking. We don't care about all the keen things your product will do until we know that *you* know what we want, why we want it and if what you're selling is what we really need in the first place. There's a word for consultants who actively and sincerely listen to Boomer buyers, the word is…rich.

"Write down what I'm saying."

> *"As I grow older, I pay less attention to*
> *what people say, I just watch what they do."*
> *— Andrew Carnegie*

It's impossible for boomers to have a high level of confidence in sales consultants who won't take notes. We know there is a 99.9% chance they won't have total recall and won't remember everything we said. If they can't remember, they won't deliver, period. If you're fortunate enough to have total recall, you still need to take notes. Why? Well, first of all, if you tell us you have total recall, our skeptical minds probably won't believe you. But more importantly, when you write down what we're saying you put us at ease, show you're paying attention and prove you care. You can't go wrong there.

"Encourage me to tell you more."

"The rests are just as important as the notes."
– Wolfgang Amadeus Mozart

We love to talk, but we're cautious of giving too much information to consultants we've just met. We're like a paramour who's been burned once too often and is now gun-shy about going on a date with you. So you'd better break out the roses. In our case, draw us out with simple statements like, "I see…", "Wow…", "And then what happened…?" Nod your head to show you're into what we're saying. Give us time to tell you more by pausing a second to two after we finish speaking. Imagine you're conducting an interview with a fascinating celebrity. People love to tell their stories; encourage us to tell ours.

This brings up another advantage of note taking: it creates a natural silence that gives us time to formulate our thoughts and feel comfortable giving you our personal information. The harder you listen, the more willing we become to give you special insight into our deepest wants, dreams and desires.

"Let me interrupt."

Never miss an opportunity to let Boomers sell ourselves.

Once boomers realize that we won't live forever, many of us try to cram more living into our remaining time. If we interrupt you in mid-sentence, we're not trying to be rude; we may just be in a hurry or want to make an important point before it slips our minds. Glance at our mouths while you're "looking us in the eye" and watch our body language for clues we want to interrupt — leaning forward, slightly raising a hand or mouthing silent words.

"Go the extra mile."

Boomers know there's no traffic jam on the extra mile.

When you do more than what's expected, you not only demonstrate you can be trusted, you create a level of confidence that eliminates many future objections. On the other hand, if you mention in passing that you'll send us a small piece of literature, but don't, an amazing degree of trust will be lost. If you say you're going to do something, do it earlier and better than you said you would. Under-promise and over-deliver every single time and Boomers will love you, because that epitomizes the "people are only as good as their word" principle that we cherish.

"Light my fire."

Confidence is trust fully wrapped with emotional satisfaction.

The farther Boomer buyers move away from the low-cost, minimum solution and towards the best-of-the-best, the greater our emotional involvement. The act of buying premium products is first and last an emotional *experience*; signing the proposal and writing a check is an emotional *response*. Your primary job is to manage our emotional experience. The emotional benefits of your solution are never entirely obvious to us, and they won't be obvious to you until you get to know our wants, needs, desires, dreams and fears. For example, if you're selling mattresses, you can't know the emotional value of a great night's sleep until you find out that a husband wakes up cranky, spoils a wonderful morning and hasn't gotten a decent rest in five years because his mattress kills his back. Once you get to know the emotional needs of the Boomer customer, you can help increase positive emotions attached to the sale while reducing negative ones.

Perhaps more than anything else, we want to feel good about our judgment in making a purchase; we want our buying decision to be evidence that we are wise shoppers who evaluate people well and drive a hard bargain. We all ask the same questions of ourselves:

- Am I buying the right product?
- Am I getting the best value?
- Am I dealing with the right person?

Confidence Disarms our "Rip-Off Prevention System"

After years of painful and expensive buying experiences, Boomers have learned that the most important element in the purchase of any product is the person selling it. As our confidence in you increases, price becomes less important, comparison shopping is less likely and the odds of us buying from you skyrocket. You become more than a salesperson, even more than a consultant. You become our guide, partner, and an ally. Once we have confidence in you, the rest is just working out the details.

The harder you listen, the smarter Boomers think you are

- Listening makes people receptive to your ideas
- Listen with the intent to hear, not to reply
- You can't know too much, but you can talk too much
- Listening is much more than hearing, it's understanding
- Listening is the key to creating confidence and closing sales
- The most important communication skill isn't talking, it's listening
- The better you listen to us, the faster we will act on your ideas
- Wealthy consultants, listen with their eyes, ears, emotion and intellect
- The #1 reason Boomers don't buy premium products is the salesperson is talking instead of listening

TWO

When desire is high, Boomers will buy.

Determine Desires

As the first Baby Boomers entered their second year of life, Jackie Robinson became the first African-American to play major league baseball. Robinson, an amazing athlete (the first person in UCLA history to letter in four sports in one year), was known for a short temper when pushed into a corner (as an army officer in Texas he was court-martialed for not moving to the back of a city bus.) He suffered torrents of verbal abuse from the fans of both teams during every game. The Cardinals threatened to strike if Robinson played, and even some members of his own team, the Brooklyn Dodgers, threatened to walk out.

The physical abuse was worse. During his first season Robinson played first base during all 151 games – the perfect place to be run over, knocked down or "accidentally" sliced up with a pair of cleats. Opposing pitchers would routinely aim for his head or intentionally hit him with a fastball. Even though he faced ridicule and danger during every game, Robinson just worked harder. In 1947, Jackie Robinson led the National League in stolen bases, hit .297 and received the first ever Rookie of the Year award. One word sums up why Jackie Robinson endured oppressive physical and emotional abuse and never quit: Desire.

— Boomer Selling Insight —
Desire is a complex emotion
that drives all Boomer behavior

We want what we want, and when we want it badly enough nothing will turn us aside. For Boomer buyers, desire is the primary emotion controlling what we buy, who we buy it from and how much money we'll spend. When serious money is involved, the sale always starts and ends with desire. Desires are usually a means to an end, not the end itself.

If Jackie Robinson's desire was to just play baseball, he could have returned to the Negro Leagues where the fans idolized him and the players respected him. He could have gone back to Canada where the players were tolerant and the fans thought he was great. But for Robinson, baseball was more than a game, it was a means to an end. Every day that he played, Jackie Robinson knew that he was one day closer to helping every African-American get the full civil rights enjoyed by white Americans.

When Boomers develop a desire to purchase a certain product or service, that desire is almost always the product of an underlying emotional need that

> **Desire is a strong need fueled by emotions**

we are trying to fulfill, often without being aware of it (the exception is the emergency purchase driven by something like a sudden car battery failure or plumbing disaster). For example, let's say you're a late-night TV watcher back in the 1970s and you see the pitch for that ridiculous stomach stimulator belt that was supposed to tone your abdominal muscles with electrical impulses, so you could get a six-pack while sitting on the couch drinking a six pack. And in a sudden impulsive rush, you buy the thing. Which is the more plausible reason:

A. You reviewed the scientific, double-blind, placebo-controlled research on the device and determined that yes, it did improve abdominal strength and conditioning;

B. Or you felt embarrassed that your middle-aged spread was getting to be the size of the ranch house in *Bonanza* and were desperate for an easy, no-exercise way to feel better about yourself?

The answer, of course, is B. Your emotional stew—comprised of humiliation over your potbelly and your hatred of exercise—made you buy something that your intellect knew had to be a scam. But that's the power of emotions in the sales process. Emotions can and do overrule reason. Why else would 50-year-old guys buy $80,000 Porsches with only two seats and no trunk space? That has nothing to do with logic or need. It's the desire to feel young and virile again that's writing the check.

We Don't Buy What We Need; We Buy What We Desire

We need food, and we could all get by for a very long time eating nothing but beans, rice and cabbage (and indeed, that's what some people did during the Depression).

But we desire greasy, artery-clogging hamburgers and fries, $30 filet mignon and butterfat-rich ice cream. The renowned behavioral psychologist Abraham Maslow said humans are rarely in a state of complete happiness; we always desire something, and as one desire is satisfied another appears. As our income goes up, we desire things we never dreamed of before. Since Boomer income is rising faster than any other demographic group, we desire more.

The savvy sales consultant turns this to his or her advantage by understanding that while Boomers may say that we're looking for certain features or solutions, what our subconscious minds are desperately seeking are things that will satisfy our emotion-based desires. We might come into your store and tell you we're looking for a basic television, but what we really want is a 60-inch plasma television with surround-sound that will make us feel like we're sitting in the Italian restaurant during the famous assassination scene in *The Godfather*—we love this stuff... and it doesn't hurt that we'll impress the heck out of our peers. Underneath every supposedly rational premium product buying quest is a desire we may not even be aware of. If you can discover what those desires are and construct solutions that satisfy them, we'll adopt you, bring you homemade cookies on the job and possibly invite you to Thanksgiving dinner with the family.

I Second That Emotion

In the heyday of the TV pitchmen, the air waves were full of hyperkinetic ads for things like Ginsu knives, the Ronco glass froster, or the pocket fisherman, or fitness guru Jack LaLanne pushing his juicing machine. Boomers all watched them and millions of us bought the products—not because we had some great practical need to saw through an aluminum can, scramble an egg while it was still in the shell or carry a fishing pole in our front pocket or purse, but because we had a desire to own something that we felt put us on the cutting edge and made us feel advanced. Somehow our lives would not be complete if we didn't call the 800 number with credit card in hand right now. Those desires, which drive all sales activity are, in turn, produced by our emotions:

- Emotions create compelling psychological needs that crave immediate satisfaction

- Emotions make up an essential part of all human decision making

- Our most important motivator isn't facts, it's feelings

- Emotional benefits are never completely obvious to the buyer or seller

- Emotional priorities are always more important than price

- The faster and deeper our emotional connection – the faster we buy and the deeper we dig into our pockets

Each desire is linked to a blend of emotional needs, so it's essential to understand how emotions create desire. Here are some of the more common desires that drive sales and the emotions that are most often behind them:

DESIRE	EMOTION
Peace of mind	Reliability, dependability, freedom from discomfort and worry. We may have a great deal of stress in our lives: children moving back home; parents moving in; health troubles; relationships ending. Peace of mind can be our strongest buying motive.
Pride	Many Boomers have moved from feelings of "I want" to "I deserve." Many of the things we buy signal our social status or preferred self-image. About 40% of Boomer buying is purely driven by ego and pride.
Prestige	Insecurity, validation, recognition, competition. Premium brands carry prestige that makes us appear wealthy and successful to others; it's more about meaning than money…a Mercedes-Benz hood ornament cost a few dollars to make but adds thousands to the price of prestige.
Profit	Desire to reach financial freedom. Insecurity about finances, fear of running out of money, longstanding habits of pinching pennies; Boomers are extremely emotional about making, saving and losing money.

The challenge is in penetrating the denial and even delusion that can lie behind strong, motivating desires and figuring out what the customer really needs in order to gain emotional satisfaction. Boomers aren't going to let you in easily; we're cantankerous and headstrong and smart and experienced, and we may not even realize what feelings are powering our desires. In every situation, know one thing:

The answer is in the question

A basic tenet of Boomer Selling is knowing what drove the person in front of you to roll out of bed, skip *Sweatin' to the Oldies*, grab a Starbucks grande latte and walk into your store or office with credit card in hand. If you're going to turn the situation into a premium sale, repeat business and solid gold referrals, then you need to know what's happening between the Boomer buyer's ears.

— *Boomer Selling Insight* —
Boomer Selling isn't just about creating new desires; it's also helping us discover the desires we already have

Two and a half thousand years ago, Aristotle taught us the secret to selling to Baby Boomers when he said, "The fool tells me his reasons; the wise man persuades me with my own." Aristotle would have made a heck of a sales consultant. Don't try to talk us into buying; you'll run out of words. Instead, ask the right questions—the right way, at the right time—then stand back and *let us sell ourselves*. You should be asking questions that are open-ended (meaning they don't lend themselves to "Yes" or "No" answers) and that lead naturally to other questions. Here's what the right questions can do:

- **Focus us**—Questions connect emotionally then capture and hold our fleeting attention.

- **Build rapport**—The more we get to talk about us, the more we tend to like you.

- **Trigger emotions**—Questions give you the ability to recognize and understand the emotions of others.

- **Create confidence**—The more you know what we want, the more confidence we have that you'll deliver.

- **Create opportunities**—Questions help you determine our wants, needs and desires—and help us do the same.

- **Learn priorities**—Our most sought-after priority may be worth 10 times more than the next most desired solution.

- **Reveal expectations**—Only when you know our expectations can you meet or exceed them.

- **Reveal fears**—Our emotions are immediately engaged when you ask about our fears, family, goals, concerns and desires.

- **Help us understand our motivations**—It's not so much about the purchase; it's what the purchase means specifically to us. We may not have thought about it until you ask.

- **Discover desires**—Because Boomers are drowning in options and unlimited choices, questions allow you and us to zero in on what's in our best interest.

- **Reduce resistance**—Boomers may hate sales tactics but we don't resist our own ideas, so the more we talk the more we sell ourselves.

Prescription Before Diagnoses is Malpractice

Most people don't get married after the first date or buy the moment they see your product. Spending serious money for premium products, just like launching a marriage, requires a series of decisions, a cognitive process. The closer your selling process matches our buying process, the more likely we are to do business with you. Two things determine how well your selling process meshes with our buying process:

1. The type of questions you ask
2. The sequence in which you ask them

If you don't ask the right questions, the results can be disastrous. Imagine you're a doctor with a patient complaining of excruciating abdominal pain. The problem could be anything from indigestion to stomach cancer. What would you do first? You'd probably do the least invasive test that provides the most useful information. If you don't get the information you need, you'd keep narrowing your focus until you did. To do otherwise would be malpractice.

Here are the four levels of diagnostic questions to ask:

1. Open with broad, "Tell me about . . ." questions.
2. Discover desires with, "What, who, how, when, where?" questions.
3. Gain "tipping-point" information with, "Why?" questions.
4. Determine priorities, eliminate competition and close the sale with, "What if...?" questions.

Converse, Don't Interrogate

There's a fine line between asking well-designed questions that feel natural to the customer and coming across like the evil dentist played by Laurence Olivier in *Marathon Man,* pulling Dustin Hoffman's teeth while hissing, "Is it safe?" If you appear that you're a police interrogator running through the standard suspect list of questions, we're going to file you away as just another sales non-professional. Your questioning should be natural, easy, respectful, and based on listening. Some guidelines:

- **Ask permission before you invade our minds—** Every Boomer has been painted into a corner with questions by some sales hack, so when you start asking questions, defenses go up faster than the deflector shields on the Starship Enterprise. To keep this from happening, tell us why it's in our best interest to answer your questions. Say something like, "There are hundreds of ways to design and install your new swimming pool, but the best way is what's best for you and your family. To find out what's best, do you mind if I ask a few questions?"

- **Give us the freedom to speak freely**—Boomers subconsciously feel we're going to get trapped when somebody asks us a pin-down, half nelson-style question. Four questions we feel safe answering (and that will get us talking so much we'll probably tell you more than we intended) are:
  "Would you tell me about...?"
  "What plans have you made to...?"
  "What are you feeling concerning...?"
  "What's been your experience with...?"

- **Discover desires with spontaneous questions**

*"I keep six honest serving men they taught me
all I knew; their names are What and Why
and When and How and Where and Who."*
– Rudyard Kipling

When your questions focus on how we can improve our lives instead of your bank account, it's much easier to share our feelings, fears, dreams and desires. Let's say your business is selling heating, ventilation and air conditioning (HVAC) systems to homeowners. The buyers gave you a general idea of what's going on, but now it's time to narrow the focus with a question like, "Does anyone (who) in your family suffer from airborne allergies or asthma?" If "no" move on, but if "yes" ask intelligent, spontaneous follow-up questions, like you do when talking to a friend:

- "What time of year are your grandson Bobby's allergies to pollen the worst?
- "Do his allergies affect how he sleeps?"
- "Does Bobby's restless sleep affect his school work or study habits?"

Your questions allowed us to discover that you're not just selling a box that blows hot and cold air; you're selling something that can help us improve the comfort and protect the health of our loved ones. Powerful stuff!

- **Ask "Why?"**—Boomers usually have two kinds of desires: the ones we tell you about and the ones we don't. We're not being coy; much of the time we don't fully understand our own desires.

(See what I mean by complex?) The best way to help you and me discover my deepest desires is to ask me, "Why?" Surprisingly, a lot of the time we've never thought about why we want a certain product or solution, and the reasons can be both complex and revealing.

When you do this, an amazing thing happens: we start telling you things we weren't even aware of and the more we tell you, the more we tend to sell ourselves. "Why" is a very tricky question to ask Boomers; if you ask before you establish the right level of confidence and trust, we'll view you as being pushy, maybe even antagonistic. To avoid this problem, tell us *why* it's in our best interest to tell you why. For instance, "To help me develop a program that best meets your financial goals, do you mind if I ask why $500 per month is the amount you want to invest?"

Here's an example of a great sales exchange between a sales consultant selling high-end home video and audio systems and a Boomer couple out to spend some serious cash:

SALES CONSULTANT: "Tell me about your entertainment space. *What* is it like?"

BOOMER CUSTOMERS: "Well, we have a finished basement with concrete pillars but otherwise, it's got dark paneling and deep carpet, very comfortable."

SC: "*Who* will be spending the most time there and *what* will they be doing?"

BC: "Both of us, and our closest friends, and we'll probably spend a lot of time watching classic movies and drinking wine." "My buddies and I will probably watch a lot of football down there during the winter." "And my girlfriends and I are looking forward to movie night once a week like Carmela Soprano."

SC: "So it's an adult playroom, essentially. Good. Let me ask you, *what* do you want to feel when you step into your media room? *What* do you want others to feel?"

BC: "I think we both want to feel comfortable and like we've given ourselves something top of the line, which we've never done before. As for our friends, I'd like them to feel wrapped in luxury, like I'm treating them to a really premium experience."

SC: "Hmm, OK. Do you mind if I ask you something personal?"

BC: "Go ahead."

SC: "Thank you. *Why* are you doing this now?"

BC: "Well, when the kids were home we were always very frugal and we weren't comfortable entertaining because we didn't feel our home was very welcoming. Now I guess we want to make up for that by creating a really lush, adult space where our friends can drink, enjoy good food and feel relaxed and comfortable."

SC: "Excellent. *What if* I were to suggest not only a top-of-the-line video and audio system, but a wine cellar and a small bistro kitchen, so you would essentially have a private café below ground just for family and friends?"

BC: "Wow. That sounds incredible. Tell me more."

High Priorities Close Sales

"My talent lies in my ability to ask very simple,
yet very powerful questions like, "What if...?"
— *Albert Einstein*

When you ask us to prioritize our needs, the big switch connecting our conscious and subconscious minds closes. All the desires that are hiding out under the radar suddenly stick their heads up like the chimney sweeps in the rooftop production number in *Mary Poppins* and say, "Hello!" All of a sudden, we're more able to articulate our desires, even if we still don't understand or even acknowledge the emotions that lie behind them, it doesn't matter. So if you ask something like, "If we could significantly reduce the airborne pollen that's affecting your grandson's allergies, would that be a high, medium or low priority?" and if you're anywhere close to the target, we're probably going to open up and tell you a lot more than you asked for.

- High priorities are conscious desires that our subconscious mind wants to take care of *now*

- Medium priorities are wants that may have the potential of becoming intense desires with a few more emotion building questions

- Low priorities are warning flags; once you know them, they can keep you from making serious mistakes by offering things we don't want

Your focus should always be on meeting our highest priorities first.

Become Fluent in Body Language

The 1960 Kennedy/ Nixon presidential debate was the first time in history voters could watch their candidates "duke it out" on television. Those who heard the debate "the old fashioned way" on their radio said Nixon won. He sounded like the man they wanted in the White House. He was articulate, his voice had the confidence of experience, and he had full

The best known study on human communication was published by UCLA and revealed:

- 7% of communication is by words

- 38% of communication is by "tone of voice"

- 55% of communication is based on body language

command of the issues. The folks who watched the debate on TV said Kennedy won by a wide margin. Why the huge difference?

Nixon was 20 pounds underweight due to a recent surgery, slouched slightly, wore a sloppy, light-colored suit, had a serious five-o'clock shadow and the pallor of a corpse because he refused to wear make-up. Kennedy was perfectly groomed, wore a tailored dark suit, stood erect, used expressive gestures and "looked the nation in the eye" when he spoke. Kennedy won because the people who watched on television focused on what they saw, not what they heard.

Emotions are accompanied by physical changes, and learning how to read these changes can give you a powerful edge in becoming an irreplaceable consultant. The word *emotion* comes from two Latin words: "ex" for *out* or *outward* and "moto" for *movement* or *motion*. Emotions are created by neurochemicals like dopamine, noradrenalin and serotonin. Among other things, these self-manufactured drugs speed up the brain's activity level, which creates changes in body movement. Positive emotions can cause involuntary physical responses like heavier breathing, increased eye contact, relaxed facial expressions and larger pupil size. If you've ever watched the World Series of Poker on television you've probably noticed many of the best players such as Chris Ferguson and Scotty Nguyen, hide their eyes with sunglasses to keep from giving away their hands with involuntary "tells." Even professional poker players can't always control their "outward motion."

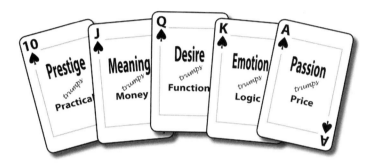

Instead of trying to focus on every change in body language (which can severely limit your ability to listen) look for subtle changes in mood and demeanor: faster speech, more excitement in the voice, interrupting the conversation to ask questions about price, warranties or availability, etc. Don't get hung up on pop psychology like "crossing the arms is a defensive gesture;" for some Boomers, crossing the arms simply reduces back pain. Don't base your sales process on body language, but use it to help guide your questions and give you valuable sign-posts to our desires.

In the end, desire trumps price. To say it another way, nothing is over-priced; it's just under-desired. If you can create or amplify our desires enough with your smart emphatic selling and discovery of our hidden emotional needs, you'll overcome price objections the vast majority of the time. Even when money is tight, Boomers buy the things we desire most. After all, we already know we deserve the best of everything!

To find out what Boomers want, ask!

- The right questions are like turning on a light in a dark room

- The most powerful method of persuasion is asking intelligent questions

- Ask questions that encourage buyers to think

- Questions help change or reinforce buyers' beliefs

- Ask to determine buyers' scope of experience

- Questions are more emotionally powerful than statements

- Learning buyers' thoughts and feelings by asking questions is more important than presenting features and benefits

- Never tell when you can ask

THREE

Customization delights Boomers,
eliminates competition and maximizes profits.

Customize Solutions

—————————

Thanks to the introduction of the Model T, the car that put America on wheels, Ford Motor Company controlled 60% of the new car market before World War I. But as America entered World War II, Ford retained less than 20% market share. What happened? How could the company that sold the lowest priced cars in the industry ($440 in 1915) lose two-thirds of a rapidly growing market in just 23 years? Henry Ford gave us the answer when he said, "People can have the Model T in any color, so long as it's black."

One of Ford's chief rivals was a man named Alfred P. Sloan. When Sloan became president of General Motors in 1923, the automaker barely held 12 percent of the new car market. Eight years later GM surpassed Ford once-and-for-all. Unlike a stubborn Henry Ford, who tried to control the market by undercutting his competitors' prices with one massed produced model, Sloan's philosophy was, "A car for every purse and purpose." Sloan knew automobiles symbolized more than transportation and buyers wanted more than a car that looked like every other one on the road. Without the aid of focus groups and opinion surveys, Sloan also knew American buyers were willing to scrimp and save to buy a car with the colors, styles and features that would satisfy both their logical needs and emotional desires, something the rational Ford apparently couldn't understand.

Under Sloan's leadership, GM established annual styling changes (now called "planned obsolescence") and a pricing structure in which buyers could move from lowest priced cars (Chevrolet and Pontiac) to highest priced (Buick and Cadillac). Buyers could also mix and match interior and exterior colors and high margin accessories like heaters and radios. When the first Boomers turned 10 in 1956, General Motors produced over half of all new cars sold in America. GM's early concept of customization, along with Ford's resistance to give buyers what they wanted, allowed GM to become the biggest and most profitable industrial enterprise the world had ever known.

Boomers Crave Customization

In the 18 years following World War II the US birth rate exploded from two million to over four million per year. The average Boomer grew up with three siblings and sat in an overcrowded classroom with 35 other children. To get noticed by overworked teachers and fit in with our like-minded peers we customized our clothes, hairstyles, language and even our attitudes. For better or worse, customization is what made Boomers the unique individuals we are today.

Today customization is so prevalent that it's mathematically impossible to find two Boomers out of the 77 million of us who use exactly

> There are 221,184 possible ways for a customer to order a Whopper® sandwich
>
> - Burger King advertisement

the same combinations of every-day products. Basic goods like toothpaste, shampoo, laundry detergent, coffee, breakfast cereal, which consumers were lucky to find on the shelves during WWII, now each come in at least 10 different versions. Our grandparents may have been the first to see the excitement of customization, but Boomers were the first to make customization the foundation of a mega-consumption lifestyle.

— Boomer Selling Insight —
Like snowflakes, no two Boomers are the same

When the first Baby Boom came along in 1946, the children of the Depression/War generation found ourselves living in the greatest time of plenty the world has ever known. Anyone with enough drive and determination could live the American Dream of financial freedom, a good job, a fine house and a shiny new car with tail fins as big as Texas—and millions of us did. Fast forward to today, and many of us choose to customize our lifestyle with major premium products from brands like Lexus, Rolex and Trane and Viking because of lessons our parents taught us during the lean times:

- "Buy cheap, buy twice"
- "You get what you pay for"
- "Only premium products provide premium benefits"

We want quality because we grew up with quality all around us. But to Boomers today, quality doesn't just mean materials and design. It means customization. We want solutions tailored exclusively to our needs, which are, of course, like no one else's. All 77 million of us are unique.

Make It Customized and Make It Good

Boomers tend to place greater-than-usual value in giving ourselves and our families the comfort and quality we feel we deserve. Will we invest our hard-earned money in a slower computer or a smaller TV with poorer sound quality, or trade down to a car with crank windows? Sure, when we can ice skate in Hades!

— Boomer Selling Insight —
When we replace just about anything, we want the
next one to be better—in most cases, much better—
even if it pinches us financially to do so

We are wired by life experience and decades of sacrifice to demand the best of the best if it's available, and
for us the best means something custom-designed for
our special needs, lifestyles, or interests. Most Boomers
reach a point in our lives where we are willing to trade
money for more time, lower risk, reduced hassles and
emotional comfort.

This demand for customization is what has made the
personal computer the ultimate growth product for the
Boomer generation and beyond. Yet just a few years ago,
we were barely wired at all, especially in comparison with
the MySpace and Facebook generation. Why the massive growth in living the wired life? One of the big reasons is the fact that computers have become the ultimate
customizable products.

Boomers remember way back when the earliest home
computers came out. Machines like the Commodore 64,
the Radio Shack TRS-80 and the Amiga seem incredibly
primitive now with their monochrome graphics and tiny
hard drives (if they even had hard drives at all.) In those
slow old days, if we wanted to get something worthwhile
out of a computer, we had to find a computer geek. But

then along came the 1990s and the Internet boom and, with them, amazing new computers from companies like Apple and Dell, powerful new software and a universe of music, movies, blogs and applications on the Internet, together with fast access. Today, a Boomer's computer can be like no one else's; in 30 minutes he or she can download "Outer Limits" reruns, fill an online music library with The Doors and Bob Dylan tunes, and bookmark a thousand wonderful websites.

The world is our customized computer, or should be. We want a limitless menu of features and options. That's what will make us your devoted customer for life.

— Boomer Selling Insight —
We choose the consultant who does the
best job of helping us customize solutions
around our unique wants, needs and desires

We're Into Legacies Now

Boomers didn't want to get into this stuff a few years back, because we were all sure we were going to live forever, or at least have our heads frozen like Ted Williams and be brought back in time for the 1000th anniversary of Woodstock or something. But then ageless wonders like George Burns and Bob Hope had to go and die, and we realized, "Hey, this is going to happen to us, too." So now we're thinking about what we're going to leave behind—or more to the point, how we're taking care of our kids and grandkids now, while we're still on the sunny side of a dirt nap.

Boomers want to build a tangible legacy to pass on to their children and grandchildren, so that makes children and grandchildren an important consideration in your selling and consultative process. Look at the research: 58% of Boomers will pay more for a home that is fun for kids and 52% will spring

> You may be talking to a younger person, but it may be their Boomer parents or grandparents paying the bill

for design features that make the home safe for children. Many Boomer parents were so busy raising our standard of living that sometimes we neglected raising our children. Because most of us have more time and money now, we refuse to let this happen with our grandchildren. There's not a grandparent alive who isn't willing to make a sacrifice for their grandkids, (and maybe assuage some of the guilt we feel for our shortcomings as parents along the way).

Boomers who waited longer to start a family than their own parents are likely to have only one child, compared to two or three just a decade or two ago. So the importance of that child is magnified. And of course, smaller families can usually afford better products with greater customization. So when it's appropriate, demonstrate how your solution suits the needs not just of the Boomer but the Boomer family unit, which may include adult kids, and grandkids from more than one marriage. Be sensitive but ask questions and find out.

Boomers Won't Postpone Gratification

Alongside Boomers' desire to provide the best for their descendants now and in the future, this generation also has a keen awareness of mortality and wants to make the most of now. We don't want to postpone gratification. Boomers are "time starved buyers." Every birthday reminds us that time is our most valuable resource. We prefer to do business with people who won't waste our time with empty sales pitches for solutions we don't need; in fact, the fastest way to earn our lifelong enmity is to make us feel that you've wasted some of our precious time trying to sell us something that's right for *you*, not for us. Don't you know there are mountain bikes to be ridden, masters tennis tournaments to be played, stereotypes to defy and foreign countries we haven't visited yet?

On the other hand, if you can give us custom yet turnkey solutions that save us time, we'll probably name one of our grandchildren after you...or at least a fish.

Compromise? Not If We Can Help It

But perhaps the most powerful draw toward customized offerings in technology, security, travel, apparel, legal services or virtually any other area of commerce has to do with Boomers' seething hatred of compromise. You see, we spent all those post-war years growing up in an era of "Leave It To Beaver" propriety and righteousness. Sex was off the table, at least publicly. Race was just an ugly issue. Whole Foods? Yeah, right. Our health food was Wonder Bread with less mayo, and only hippies and kooks ate yogurt or did yoga. Why do you think we went so nuts when the sixties and seventies came along?

Early Boomers compromised on our urges in the '50s, cut loose in the '60s, and then came the '70s with gas wars, unemployment and inflation. Back to compromise. In the '80s and '90s every Boomer discovered that many of the jobs we thought we would have for life were sent overseas or eliminated altogether. To make a long story short, Boomers have spent many years doing without or suppressing what we wanted, and we're done with that. We want to drink deep of the wine of life, even if it comes in a two-liter box. We're sick of compromising and settling for what everyone else has. That's why Boomers are the leading subscribers to "concierge" healthcare, where instead of seeing all patients, doctors maintain a smaller base of top patients who can afford to pay as much as $15,000 a year for private, personal, *customized* care.

— Boomer Selling Insight —
The happier we are, the more we buy,
and the more we buy, the happier *you* are

We want to feel that we're getting something special, that we're exceptional shoppers. We want a buying experience that leaves us buzzed and fired up, like we just finished our third pot of double caffeine espresso. Buying large ticket items can be a fun, exciting and emotionally-charged experience for you and us. Our enthusiasm for the best of the best is infectious. The more excited you are about giving us a solution that's tailored precisely to what we need and crave, focusing on premium quality experience, the more pleasure we receive.

> **"People have a burning passion to be better off today than yesterday and better tomorrow than today"**
>
> - Abraham Maslow

There's another, very powerful aspect to customization. The more complex the product, the more compromises the buyer may be asked to make—and boy, are today's products complex! Where once you had color versus black-and-white TV, now you have HDTV, plasma, LCD, projection and so on. Where once you had hardtop versus convertible cars, now you have hybrids, SUVs, electric cars and smart cars. Even simple choices like what to eat and what to wear have become dizzying. And the fact is, when customers feel uninformed about a complex purchase, they will feel forced to compromise toward the center, where they feel that they are most likely to find a mediocre blend of bland quality and ho-hum value. But what if you could be that consultant who brings all your knowledge to bear in showing us how the perfect solution can be customized to give us *exactly* what we need and want? We will usually default to the more expensive choice if it gives us what we know we desire and deserve, because we were raised on the idea of enduring value. Customization provides that value.

Don't be surprised if things like appearance, style and snazzy features—the stuff that dazzles friends—are what make the sale. I never said we weren't vain. The point is, once Boomers understand that you are giving us the information and understanding we need to *collaborate* with you in creating a solution that's unique to us, we'll never comparison shop again.

For example, a Boomer went to a computer store looking for help. She had little familiarity with computers, but wanted to be able to e-mail her grandchildren, who were scattered all over the country. After some pointed questions about equipment, the sales consultant determined that the woman was seriously uncomfortable using tools like web cameras, so he directed her to an Apple laptop with a built-in camera and software that would allow her to do three-way live video calling with her grandkids. He sealed the deal by going out to his car and getting his own Apple laptop and showing her software that would allow her to make low-cost, Internet-based phone calls to her grandchildren, and this sense of collaboration allowed him to sell the delighted Boomer not only a $2,500 laptop but a photo printer, DVD burner and high-speed Internet service.

Boomers at all income levels selectively purchase premium products

Boomers view ourselves in different roles at different times: father; grandfather; coach; community leader; department manger, etc. Each role shapes our behavior and attracts us to products that are consistent with that behavior. Research shows it is easier for the buyer to distinguish the "right" things to buy when the product is linked directly to the role.

Role: *Serious Boomer Mountain Biker*
Funds: *Limited*
Requirements: *Reliable brakes*
Choices: *Weenie Pride ($60), Pucker-Factor ($180)*

Which brakes do you think Serious Boomer Biker bought? Even though Weenie Pride would meet the requirements, why did Serious Boomer Biker pay three times more for Pucker-Factor brakes? It wasn't because they stop a fraction of a second quicker or weigh seven grams less; it was because Weenie Pride would have shattered Serious Boomer Biker's self image. Even though it was the best choice for the funds available, Weenie Pride was never considered.

The Heart of Your Selling Strategy

Customization is more work, to be sure. It's easier and faster for you to sell someone a solution "off the rack" and straight out of the box. But Boomers don't want that; we pride ourselves on being one-of-a-kind, and we want (sometimes demand) solutions that fit us like our favorite pair of faded Levis. But cheer up—customization isn't that hard, and it gives you the opportunity to add major profit potential to each transaction. The eight reasons to customize are:

1. Customization Creates An Emotional Connection

Boomers share a common need for customizing everything, from the vehicle we drive, our home color schemes, our cell phone ring tones, the fast food meals we pick up on the way home and virtually everything else. This personalization creates a greater sense of emotional bonding with your customized solution, your company and you. Ever ask yourself why Apple computer users have such intense, lifelong loyalty? It's not just that the products are great; it's that they are easily personalized, especially products like the iPod, which basically becomes a canvas for reflecting the individual's musical tastes. The Volkswagen Beetle had the same kind of cache.

— Boomer Selling Insight —
We don't buy what it is;
we buy how it makes us feel

Customization creates what marketers call *affinity*, which means that Boomers go beyond liking your company or trusting you to having a deep and lasting emotional connection to you—a belief that you really do care and want what is best for us. You know how powerful a selling tool that is.

2. Customization Increases Premium Sales...and Profits

Less than 20% of all Boomers buy the lowest-cost-entry-level-solutions. Those who do usually do so out of a lifelong habit of frugality or lack of desire or because that's all they can afford. The rest of us? We want the benefit-packed option, please.

Most manufacturers try to capture as much market share as possible by producing several versions of a similar product. At the bottom end of the scale is the "entry level" model that does little more than its core function. This would be a Toyota Corolla, for example, or a three-day Mexico cruise on "The Love Boat." Then we pass various entry-level upgrades and mid-level options until we get to the top of the scale: premium products. This is where you find the tightest sealing windows and the most durable ATV's.

> **The fastest, easiest and most reliable way to increase customer satisfaction is to sell more premium products**

The odd thing is that even though the entry-level version is the least expensive for consumers to buy, it's the most expensive for businesses to sell. It takes the same space to transport, store and deliver and process a premium product as it does its entry-level rival. So of course, all smart business owners would rather sell the premium product, and the beauty is that after years of settling for the off-the-line Corolla or vanilla Camry, Boomers are salivating for the Lexus with all the options and a color scheme they can select at the factory. So when it comes to Boomer consumers, offer the premium solutions, please. We want them, and so do you. Why? Because:

Premium products deliver premium profits

When you provide customized premium benefits that buyers want and that your competitors don't provide, the laws of supply and demand allow you to reap substantial profits. Check out these numbers:

	Typical Sale	**Premium Sale**
	$4,000	$7,000
Sales commission	- 400	- 700
Overhead	- 1,200	- 1,200
Cost	- 2,000	- 3,700
Net Profit	**$ 400**	**$1,400**

Higher profits allow businesses to hire the best people, provide the best training, and deliver support and service that consistently exceed client expectations, and that is the key to repeat business, referrals and a constant stream of future profits.

3. Customization Increases Luxury Sales

"I can easily be satisfied with the very best."
— *Winston Churchill*

One of the basic tenets of the Boomer Selling process is "Offer the solution that best meets the buyer's needs without trying to figure out if we can afford it." When you start with the best solution, you will inevitably sell more luxury products. Luxury is the best of the best that is available to you to sell. It's a product at the highest end of the quality scale that can easily cost several times more than the entry-level solution. This is what we love. This is what many of us feel that a lifetime of hard work and sacrifice has entitled us to.

Americans are buying luxury goods and services four times faster than our level of spending on non-luxury items. The new luxury goods market is worth $500 billion annually. While the demand for luxury goods is growing at 15% per year, the number of consultants who understand how to satisfy the demanding requirements of Boomer buyers' luxury needs is limited.

— Boomer Selling Insight —
Luxury isn't about money;
it's about meaning

Remember the question process we discussed earlier? Start there. Get to know your Boomer customer. Understand his or her lifestyle and self-image. If you can give us a positive unique experience that suggests you understand what makes us special, you can sell luxury. You are not just selling an architectural metal roof, premium accounting services or the ultimate water purification system, you are also selling an experience. Five-star restaurants don't make money by selling food; people can get food from

The Olive Garden. They create a multi-sensory "dining experience" that is unlike any other, and that's the way they capture the imagination and loyalty of the diner.

Luxury is a concept. Luxury buyers can always buy something that will do the job somewhere else for less money. But it isn't about money for luxury-minded Boomers. It's about rewarding ourselves for a life well lived. Luxury isn't about function, but fantasy. And for you, the huge profit produced by luxury sales is a delicious reality.

4. Customization Boosts "Add-On" Profits

"A body in motion tends to stay in motion."

– Sir Isaac Newton

One of the exciting aspects of customization is that the level of buyer excitement grows as we get really involved in the transaction. Once we decide to buy a customized, premium product, it's much easier for us to justify buying the accessories, options and add-ons that can drastically increase the benefits we receive—and supercharge your bottom line.

When you sell not only the core product (let's say it's a new swimming pool), but the optional, ancillary products that allow Boomer buyers to customize their solution (such as a DE filter, waterfall feature, tiled fish and turtle character on the pool bottom), bottom line profits and commission checks skyrocket, because you're adding sales income without increasing overhead. A portion of every core sale covers overhead, which includes advertising, utilities, rent, clerical support, insurance and so on. When you sell add-ons, business overhead is already accounted for. The result is pure profit, baby.

The JATO Effect

JATO stands for "Jet Assisted Take Off." In Viet Nam, the C-123 "Provider" aircraft delivered millions of pounds of lifesaving materials like medical supplies, food, and ammunition to U.S. soldiers and allied forces. But like a business weighted down with overhead, a fully loaded C-123 doesn't exactly leap into the sky; at best it lumbers its way up to altitude. This is not a good thing when people are shooting at you. The answer to this prickly problem was JATO: little jets strapped to the wings that created amazing thrust and got the bird into the sky much faster. Add-on sales are JATO for your business, allowing you to create an amazing boost to profits and commissions when sales increase and overhead doesn't.

Say your firm's overhead is 30%. Once overhead is covered, everything you sell is worth 30% more:

Overhead (paid)	30%
Profits from sale	$1,000
JATO effect	130%
New profits	$1,300

Your core sale pays your overhead, but you're selling thousands of dollars more worth of products and services to the same customer without spending an extra cent on marketing, lead acquisition, training or anything else. It's beautiful.

> **Customizing makes selling easy and buying fun**

5. Customization Reduces Competition

A customized solution is a "package" of your related products, accessories and services combined to provide Boomers with precisely the benefits, results and experiences we want, need and desire. Even if another customer ordered the exact same package, it doesn't matter; the individual feels that they got something unique to their lifestyle. And once we as demanding Boomer buyers realize the only way to get exactly what we want is with your customized solution, competitors have no chance.

— Boomer Selling Insight —
Customization makes true
comparison-shopping impossible

For Boomers, the cost is more than the price; it's also the cost of shopping around, the gasoline and time and trouble it takes to endure the sales pitches of multiple salespeople. Boomers may have time, but we hate to waste it. When we don't have to shop multiple sources to find what we need, we simply won't. Price ceases to matter as much as the idea that, "This company knows what I need and always provides it quickly and without hassles." That's a powerful loyalty builder.

6. Customization Reduces Objections

At the beginning of the Second World War some American fighters didn't have the power to engage enemy airplanes at high altitude, which is not a good thing when you're being chased by a German ME 109. But by replacing stock engines with ones that used exhaust gas to compress air needed for combustion, engineers created "turbocharged" American aircraft that had more power at 25,000 feet than the old engines had at takeoff. Scratch one Luftwaffe and questions about who would be the dominant air power.

As aviation engineers worked on customizing the turbocharger, no one said, "It's too expensive," "We can't afford it," or "Let's find something cheaper." We know there is a direct relationship between price, customization, reliability and quality. All smart Boomers believe quality is never an extravagance and most of us are willing to pay for it.

— Boomer Selling Insight —
Exceeding expectations is the key to
repeat business, referrals and profits

As a result, when you sell a custom, premium solution, you may earn yourself a more demanding customer, but what you won't get is a litany of baseless, time-wasting complaints from people who want something for nothing. If you can manage expectations by making it clear that customization also means on-going preventive maintenance or updating technology from time-to-time to maintain optimal performance, you can actually make customers grateful for service fees.

> **Boomers demand superior reliability and premium performance more than any other group of buyers**

7. Customization Reduces Everyone's Stress

If you focus all of your time and energy offering your entire product line to every buyer, you'll be stressed, frustrated and poor. Save your health and energy by making customizing benefits a way of life. Developing a custom package is challenging and enjoyable for the best consultants, and knowing there's a fat commission check waiting at the end of the transaction doesn't hurt, either.

8. Customization Drives Future Business

Nothing maximizes Boomer satisfaction or exceeds expectations like customization. We're conditioned these days to expect companies to treat us like cattle, so when you take the time to develop a solution that's truly based on an intimate understanding of our needs and lifestyle, you'll blow us away. Boomers grew up with great expectations and any firm that can exceed our expectations is the one we'll do business with again and tell our friends about. The single best way to exceed our expectations is to customize the best solution around our individual requirements.

When dealing with Boomers, take the advice of George Bernard Shaw, "Do not do unto others as you would have them do unto you, their tastes are not the same."

Facts about premium solution Boomer buyers:

- Skeptical
- Assertive
- More sophisticated
- Competitive
- Concerned about security
- Concerned about privacy
- Want to be in control
- Fear embarrassment
- Hate uncertainty
- Value order
- Seek stability

- Demand improved performance
- Gain approval
- Be socially accepted
- Avoid risks
- Make smart investments
- Protect their family
- Defend their home
- Take care of "Self"
- Enhance quality of life
- Receive full value for money
- Do research before buying

FOUR

If risks are too high, Boomers can't buy.

R e d u c e   R i s k

Boomers grew up with the biggest risk of all, that of sudden nuclear annihilation. Have you seen the cliché image of crew cut schoolboys and pigtailed girls with bows in their hair diving underneath their desks in 1950s "civil defense" atomic bomb drills? That's based on fact. Older Boomers still remember the old "duck and cover" routine, or in the vernacular of the day, "put your head between your knees and kiss your butt goodbye." It was as much a part of our formative years as Howdy Doody, Roy Rogers and Elvis Presley.

The closest we came to an actual nuclear catastrophe was on April 26, 1986, after we were all grown up but with much more to lose: families; homes; careers. That was the day Reactor #4 at Chernobyl (a dot on the map in the then-Soviet Union) exploded, spewing more than 30 times as much radioactive fallout as was produced at Nagasaki and Hiroshima into the skies to drift as far away as eastern North America.

The worst nuclear accident in history occurred during a non-critical test to determine how long a reactor's turbines would continue to operate in the event of an unplanned shutdown. What happened next made Gilligan and the Skipper look like rocket scientists: Automatic safety controls were disconnected to prevent them from interfering with the experiment. Power output was lowered too much at the start of the test, so technicians attempted to bring it up by quickly removing *four times* too many control rods, which starting a runaway reaction that dangerously overheated the entire system. To counteract the overheated condition, engineers turned on *all* water circulation pumps, far exceeding recommended flow rates. A tremendous power surge was triggered when the excessive mass of cold water slammed into the superheated reactor. The result was a massive explosion that blew off the sides and roof of the reactor structure. The fire burned for *twelve days*. Yeah, we know all about risk.

Boomers grew up in an era of risk-taking. Being drafted for an unpopular war, civil rights protests, drug experimentation, free love and the Nixon administration all carried unique risks. But as Boomers grew older and a bit wiser, risk reduction became an important part of everyday life. As people usually do with time, we become more conservative in our approach to life as we get older. We started to see risk as something for a younger generation, something that we wanted in small measures and only if we had the right amount of insurance to protect us. In other words, we became *risk-averse*. This is the attitude you're dealing with as a sales professional. We're smart and very, very wary.

We Want a Safety Net

One of the most important factors in the Boomer's preoccupation with risk has to do with the rise of Asian goods in the U.S. economy. Back when we were growing up, Made in America was a source of pride. What else was there? We were buying Buicks with Power-Flite transmissions, RCA televisions with ten-inch screens that made optometrists happy but let us watch *Sea Hunt* in the comfort of home, Keds and Buster Brown shoes sewn by hair-netted ladies in factories in suburban Pittsburgh and Chicago. We had faith that these were the best products of their kind in the world, and what did we know? The only things we saw from "China" were fireworks imported from Taiwan.

But then came—in no particular order—the Edsel, an oil embargo, the transistor, Toyota cars, Honda motorcycles, and Japanese efficiency. American cars seemed to break down all the time and, as gas prices rose in the 1970s, the Japanese appeared to corner the market on fuel-efficient cars that ran forever. Unlike our parents, who still have clear memories of World War II and a desire to promote American-made goods, many Boomers had no misgivings about buying reliable Asian imports. Remember, we were the Vietnam generation; if the USA said, "Buy this, it's good for America," some Boomers would buy foreign out of spite. Gradually, all the premium products that Boomers wanted in order to live the "good life"—cars, electronics, computers—became available at higher quality for less money from Asia.

American business knew it had to do something, and in the proud tradition of addressing the symptom while ignoring the disease, we decided we would soften the risk of buying a junky American car or TV. The new Chrysler Corporation CEO, Lee Iacocca, identified the problem of mistrust in American cars and launched a nationwide advertising campaign offering a five-year, 50,000-mile "bumper-to-bumper" warranty on all new Chrysler vehicles. General Motors caught on and soon upped the ante to six years or 60,000 miles. Believing risk reversal was his greatest sales tool, Iacocca trumped GM's warranty with an unheard of seven-year, 70,000-mile "bumper to bumper" guarantee.

Of course, the downside of the "warranty wars" was that they confirmed what Boomers already figured: Many American cars were junk and needed such comprehensive warranty protection to shield us from the inevitable breakdown. But the Detroit warranty frenzy also set in motion a long-term trend: the demand by Boomers for a risk safety net with almost everything we buy. Today, warranties and guarantees are just the tip of the risk reversal iceberg. If you want to consistently sell to the folks who buy the vast majority of high margin premium products and services, you must:

1. Understand how Boomers perceive risk

2. Be ready, willing and able to reduce each risk to our acceptable level

3. Realize that the more risk you take, the more money you make

Boomers' Beliefs about Risk

After 9/11, millions more Americans drove to their destinations than flew, because of the anxiety involved with boarding a commercial airliner. As a result, there were 1,600 more traffic-related deaths in 2002 than in 2001. Statistically, driving as a means of travel is about 1,000 times more dangerous than flying, yet we *perceive* the risk of flying as greater, largely because we're not in control and we don't understand the incredibly complex aerodynamics that keep a jet in the air (like anyone but an engineer can understand today's cars!), but driving *feels* safer. Our analysis of risk is not exactly rational, so it's important that you understand just what our risk-related thinking is before you can develop a sales approach that turns it to your advantage. Some of Boomers' key attitudes toward risk:

- **Boomers believe trust reduces risk**—Every time we buy an unfamiliar or complex product or deal with a new company, we are taking new risks. Every detail we don't understand creates an element of risk, whether it's warranted or not. Part of creating trust means informing us about the product so that we know the potential risks and understand how you'll deal with them should they arise. The more we trust you, the less we fear risk.

- **Boomers believe premium products lower risks**—We trust premium products more and assume they give us higher quality. A recent study showed that when consumers drank identical glasses of wine, the people who were told their wine was five times more expensive than the other wine also rated the wine as much better tasting. So premium really does translate to quality, and quality for us means reduced risk of failure and poor performance.

- **Our desire to avoid risk is usually stronger than our desire for gain**—This is borne out by research that shows investors are more motivated by the possibility of losing money in the market than by the potential for gaining it.

In other words, the threat of pain is more powerful than the promise of gain. So you have to make us feel safe before you start telling all the benefits. This also means that a recommendation not to buy a certain product will be more effective than a recommendation to buy something else.

- **Most Boomers believe buying proven brands lowers risks**—Boomers actually visualize the consequences of buying one brand over another. The higher the perceived risk of a certain brand, the more likely we are to evaluate other brands that come to mind. This is why by the time Boomers hit their 40s and 50s, we have built up deep brand loyalty in certain categories such as staples, cars and travel. Known brands equal predictability, and predictability reduces our perceived risk.

- **Boomers tend to imitate others to minimize risk**—Every Boomer remembers the "Let Mikey try it…he likes it, hey Mikey!" commercial for Life cereal (that freckled kid probably put himself through graduate school on the proceeds from that commercial). The two brothers wait for their little brother to confirm that the cereal is "safe" to try. We tend to be more comfortable with a purchase when others have vetted it for us ahead of time.

- **Desire trumps risk**—The strength of our desires can overshadow our risk perception. Remember, desire trumps everything, but sometimes your job is to create the desire that compels us to take the risk. The risk of not getting exactly what we want can trump most other risks.

- **Boomers don't view all risk the same way**—It depends on the individual lifestyle and health. Some Boomers are extremely active and will view the potential failure of a leisure-related product as a major risk, while others who are more stay-at-home will be more apt to worry about a refrigerator or home heating system.

- **Negotiated sales are rife with risk**—The more negotiation involved in the sales process, the more our perceived risk ratchets up. We believe that buying negotiated products or services, like automobiles, attorneys' fees and home repairs, carry widespread risk. We're always wondering where and how you're taking us. It's important in such cases to offer total transparency and avoid any sales pressure.

- **Boomers are suspicious of "limited" warranties**—This is especially true where reliability or performance is critical. Every Boomer has been hung out to dry by warranty exclusions: nonsense like 30-day waiting periods on home warranties; computers that must be sent back to the factory in their original packaging, and hidden deductibles that cost as much as the repair. Giving us no small print, support after the sale, and no tricky clauses go a long way to reduce this perceived risk.

The Simple Equation

However, the fundamental driver of our perception of risk is basically the same as everyone else's: the more it costs or the less we can afford it, the greater the risks we perceive. As you deal with Boomers whose incomes are lower than the average, you'll find this need for reducing uncertainty becomes greater. When we're at the outer edge of what we can spend, we know our margin for error is microscopic. We can't afford to buy the wrong thing and be stuck with it. So we're looking to you to help us make the right choice for our full range of reasons: lifestyle; goals; fears; family; feelings of entitlement, and so on.

We know it's impossible to totally eliminate risk. For instance, we know the only way to totally eliminate the possibility of computer hacking is to unplug our computer, and we're not willing to do that. So what we want you to do is not do away with risk, but make us feel that our risk of making the wrong decision has been *minimized* to an acceptable level. Here's an example: I know of a Boomer couple who, after their last child left for college, decided to install gorgeous bamboo flooring throughout their house as part of a major remodel. However, after the initial consultation with the flooring company, they realized something: they would have to install the flooring before they moved in all the new furniture they were buying, of course, but the process of moving in all the heavy furnishings would surely scratch and mar their expensive floor. They were on the verge of cancelling the sale because of this.

However, the sales manager for the flooring company did a smart thing. He offered them an improvised "Mint Condition" guarantee, saying that if anything damaged the floor's finish within the first 12 months after installation, his company would come out and restore it to installation condition at no charge. This instantly reduced the Boomer couple's risk to zero, and they made the purchase. The sales consultant even had his graphics department create a certificate for this Mint Condition guarantee and send it

> According to a Yale University study, the 12 most persuasive words in the English Language are: you; money; save; new; results; easy; health; safety; love; discovery; proven; guarantee. How many relate to risk?

to the customer, and now the guarantee is part of the company's standard package.

Boomers hate the fact that there is always uncertainty in buying. We seek to reduce doubt, discomfort and regret from buying mistakes, so as you decrease our uncertainty through education, asking smart questions, learning more about us, and being transparent about the pros and cons of any solution, you'll see a corresponding increase in our confidence.

Types of Risk Boomers Face

- **Physical risk**—Pioneering psychologist Abraham Maslow, creator of the "hierarchy of needs," knew that people could not shift their attention to attaining psychological or emotional comforts until they were confident that their physical needs—food, clothing shelter, safety, sex—were met. That's no less true today than in his time. Our safety and the safety of our loved ones is our highest priority. If something's not safe and reliable, fancy features don't matter. Safety plays a role in every Boomer buying decision, but many of us may not be conscious of this powerful fear.

In Boomers' buying behavior, there's a "hierarchy of risk" that must be dealt with, and physical safety trumps all else. Our subconscious mind has an overpowering need to know how your customized solution will reduce potential safety-related risks. To eliminate anxiety caused by physical risk, point out how specific features reduce that risk, such as anti-scald controls on shower fixtures or anti-electrocution devices on GFI electrical receptacles. Even though competing products may have the same safety features, the one who mentions them first owns them.

- **Psychological risk**—What are some of our greatest fears? Feeling foolish, feeling like a sucker, feeling like we made a stupid decision. We have come to this point in life with a strong sense of our savvy, our own control over our lives, and we don't want that shaken. Boomers are voracious consumers of insurance products; maybe that's why three of the seven oldest companies in America just happen to sell insurance. We know that perceived risk is usually much higher than the actual risk of getting into a car accident or dying of cancer, but most Boomers would have serious trouble sleeping at night without life, auto and health insurance. We fear feeling like suckers and wasting our money almost as much as we fear disease or disability.

Often overlooked risks include the wrong:

- Model
- People
- Solution
- Product
- Materials
- Company
- Consultant
- Installation

The higher our desire for something, the less risk comes into play. Psychological risk manifests itself as unpleasant emotions that disturb our sense of well-being. Anytime we suspect a pending purchase could result in the feelings of guilt, remorse, regret or irresponsibility, there's a degree of psychological risk that must be resolved before we'll feel comfortable buying.

— Boomer Selling Insight —
Buyer's remorse is unresolved psychological risk

One reason Boomers buy warranties isn't because we can't afford future problems, it's because if we do have a problem we don't want to regret not being protected. This complex behavior is especially true when we purchase long-lasting, big-ticket premium products.

Before you can be successful selling to boomers you must deal with our "big ticket phobia"—our terror of being wrong when buying a seldom-purchased expensive item like a boat, recreation vehicle or home comfort system. Placate our sense of risk by:

- Knowing that we feel it
- Understanding the reasons behind it
- Addressing each risk with facts, openness, education and insight

Every time our subconscious mind wants something, it erases a little bit of perceived risk so it can justify getting what it wants. Remember, buying premium products and services is emotion-driven, with intellect and reason serving only to justify what we want in our gut. It's important as a sales consultant to keep in the back of your mind the truth that everyone who approaches you about a big-ticket item is walking on a tightrope between excitement of desire on one side and the risk of regret on the other.

Risk is like the blades of a Ninja Throwing
Star, each one has the ability to kill the sale

- **Functional risk**—Our perceived risk of a functional problem is almost always greater than the probable risk. Remember how folks think air travel is more dangerous than auto travel when it's actually 1000 times safer? Our worry about the things we own failing is far out of proportion to the likelihood of their failure. That's true in every area of commerce. How do you think insurance companies got the money to buy so many skyscrapers?

> **Boomers are more likely to replace mechanical products before they break than any other group of buyers**

Over the years we've discovered that functional risk is inevitable. The wet spot under the hot water heater will become a flood. The furnace filter we forgot to change will cause a $1,500 repair. The strange noise coming from our car's engine will leave us stranded on the freeway during rush-hour traffic. We've learned our lessons. We would rather spend the money now than deal with the disaster (and avoid the feelings of foolishness, helplessness and regret) that come later. It's like preventive medicine for the pocketbook and ego.

We know the weakest link fails first, so we rely on you to tell us what the weakest link is and what steps we can take to mitigate potential problems. Put reliability of your customized solution in its proper perspective. If your competition is bragging about 95% reliability, remind us that 95% reliable equals one day broken down per month.

Tell us why your design and the quality of all the components are what really determines your reliability and *our* peace of mind. Almost every industry has certain design standards. If you're selling a bathroom or kitchen remodel, tell us if the fixtures you sell meet ASME (American Society of Mechanical Engineers) standards, meaning they should still be working after 250,000 on-off cycles. Determine the design standards for the products you're selling and tell us how they benefit us.

Don't just hand us a piece of sales literature; point out the major components and briefly mention what makes each one reliable. Show how it's tested. Use pictures or diagrams to point out special or beefed-up features. Spend a minute or two explaining how reliability equals money (how functional risk can lead to financial risk) and how we will keep more of it with your customized solution.

— Boomer Selling Insight —
The best investment is the one with the lowest risk

• **Financial risk**—As you already know, Boomers are passionate about money and the more we view expensive items as "investments" in our comfort, our future, our safety, resale value, health and a myriad of other things, the better we like it and the more we give ourselves permission to buy. Hey, it really didn't cost anything — it was an investment. (See what I mean being complex?)

We fear paying too much, being taken advantage of and not getting everything we want, because those are the consumer equivalent of investing in a gold mine promoted by Tony Soprano or an ill-advised real estate speculation on Love Canal.

— Boomer Selling Insight —
The wrong sales process can create insurmountable risk

Consultants who use the wrong sales process can burden the entire transaction with a debilitating sense of financial risk. Take the old "Good, Better, Best" sales process. This three-choice sales system was developed to help inexperienced salespeople sell higher margin products like tires and batteries to our parents following the severe rationing enacted during WWII. Great, but we're not our parents, so why do salespeople persist in doing this? By offering three versions of the same product, salespeople psychologically draw consumers away from the least expensive (good) and most expensive (best) choices and pull them towards the middle choice (better.) Behavioral psychologists call the act of being drawn to the middle option "compromise choice." In essence, it's a process that tries

Additional ways Boomers reduce risk:

- Search the internet
- Read product information and warranties
- Ask about return policy
- Ask about "extras" and hidden costs
- Read testimonials
- Call people on your referral list
- Shop for certain safety features
- Ask about after sale service/tech support
- Watch demonstrations

to avoid risk on either end—buying cheap stuff that doesn't last or buying the expensive take-it-or-leave-it option we didn't want. On top of that the middle option was a compromise and Boomers *hate* to compromise!

It's foolish to embrace a sales process designed to pull buyers away from premium products. With the limited choice "Good, Better, Best" sales process Boomers know two things: we're either paying for something included in the package that we don't want or we're buying something that doesn't include everything we do want. Neither is a way to gain our lasting satisfaction.

Instead of giving us the same generic three choices, help us develop the *right* choice for our unique needs. Ask smart questions, listen, then customize a solution that truly meets all our requirements. As long as the price includes the elements that mitigate the risk, we'd be crazy not to go for it. Remember, for most Boomers the biggest financial risk is not getting everything we want.

• **Social Risk**—A young man met a distinguished looking woman at a cocktail party and asked what she did for a living. The woman said she was a Rolex executive. The brash young man said, "I have a Seiko that keeps time as good as any Rolex ever made." The executive said, "That may be true, but at Rolex we're not in the time-keeping business, we're in the luxury business."

When dealing with the 40% of Boomers concerned with reducing social risk, you're also in the luxury business. The luxury brands they buy are your biggest clue. If they have a Sub-Zero refrigerator in their kitchen, a Louis Vuitton on their arm or a Patek Philippe on their wrist, they'll probably appreciate your help buying "the best socially acceptable solution."

The risk here is one of not "keeping up with the Joneses." Back in that day, it might have meant buying a VW microbus when your friends were buying nice, suburban-style Roadmasters, or having one of those refrigerators whose freezer became an ice floe while everyone else seemed to buy the frost-free model.

You can become the consultant who addresses the Boomer's need for social standing. Briefly detail your brand's history, relate a story about a well-known person who bought from you, or tie your brand into a luxury brand that the Boomer customer already owns by saying something like, "This is the Rolex of exercise equipment." This helps reduce perceived social risk and gives us permission to buy the best you're selling.

> Today, being a social outcast might mean driving a gas-hungry SUV in an eco-conscious area

It's Not About Price

Bill Clinton said "It's the economy, stupid." Well, it's the risk, not the cost. Unresolved risks create insurmountable objections in the minds of Boomers that have nothing to do with the price tag. A significant number of Boomers who don't buy say the problem was the price. But that's disingenuous. In reality, the reason isn't really that your solution costs too much money, it's that the perceived risk is too high to overcome the price. If the risk is too high, *the price will be too high no matter how low the cost.* The key to boosting Boomers sales isn't lowering your price, it's lowering our concerns about the kinds of risks we've discussed in this chapter.

Unresolved risk invites comparison shopping. However, when you customize a solution that best meets our logical, emotional and risk reductions needs, we know it's a waste of time to shop around because it's impossible for us to find another consultant who even comes close to providing the value you do.

A Risk Glossary

· Risk: The likelihood of bad things happening

· Physical risk: Danger to people, buildings, animals and environment

· Risk avoidance: A decision not to become involved in a risky situation

· Risk perception: How boomers perceive threats, real and imagined

· Risk capital: The money buyer can afford to lose

· Risk reduction: Decrease in the likelihood of occurrence or consequences of an event

· Safe: An acceptably low tolerable level of risk

· Warranty: Perceived transfer of risk from the consumer to the manufacturer or retailer

FIVE

Excitement and emotions (not features and facts)
drive all Boomers' premium purchases.

Elevate Emotions

The radio crackled. "Psy-ops this is Stainless Steel, over."

"Stainless Steel, Psy-ops, over."

"Psy-ops, we have suspected Victor Charlie Hospital in area, would you come down low and slow to help us locate, over?"

"Roger that Stainless."

I was 19 years old, sitting in the right seat of a U-10, the slowest plane in the Air Force. I had three tasks: kick out psychological warfare leaflets; play pre-recorded tapes into a huge speaker; and try not to throw up.

"Psy-ops, you're taking beaucoup small arms fire." Suddenly, the calm voice changed to a scream. "PULL UP, PULL UP, PULL UP, you're taking 50 cal, for God's sake, PULL UP!" Let me just say there's nothing like being a teenager on the wrong end of hostile fire to immediately elevate your emotions.

Boomers have always craved some form of emotional stimulation. The movie industry made fortunes ratcheting up our emotions with chainsaws, horse heads and hockey masks. Amusement parks prospered by maximizing the number of g-forces our bodies could endure. Bungee jumping, mountain biking and shark feeding are activities born to meet our ever-present need for emotional stimulation. So it should come as no wonder that successful selling must include a strong strategy for appealing to the more emotional angels of our nature.

Boomers Are Emotional Buyers

"There are always two reasons people have for doing everything, the reason they state and the real reason."

– J.P. Morgan

The fact is, we're all emotional buyers. Brand development and marketing specialists know this and have exploited it for decades as our consumer culture has mushroomed: people buy with their emotions, then backward-justify their decision with their intellect and information.

For example, the average man shopping for a new car will talk about fuel economy, horsepower, crash test results and power train reliability, but he'll base 75% of his choice on how the car's doors sound when they close, how the leather seats feel, the car's profile in the showroom and other details that have nothing to do with performance or future repair costs. But after he decides, "I love this car, I must have it," he will self-approve his gut decision by talking about its practicality and any other benefit that might make it an allowable purchase in his mind. He might walk into the showroom looking for a fuel efficient 6 cylinder Chevrolet minivan, but he'll drive away in a fully loaded 295-HP Chevy Tahoe. Why? Because somehow the massive engine reminds him of the cherry-red 1973 Mustang fastback with the Boss 351 engine that he drove during his senior year in college when he made the varsity baseball team and dated a cheerleader. We are all emotional buyers, which is why fit and finish and packaging and branding can be as important as quality and service...and maybe more so.

As Boomers go through life, emotional stimulation plays an even greater role in our ever-changing communication styles and decision-making processes. Over time, the way we buy changes from the Sgt. Joe Friday routine on Dragnet—"Just the facts, ma'am"—to an intuitive buying process that uses emotion to help us make better buying choices. We frequently transition from the façade of being information-based buyers to saying, "The heck with it, I want it, I've earned it, I like it, here's my Visa." But you can't just push any emotional Boomer button and get the sale. We hate being manipulated. You've got to know how to guide us in the right direction.

It's About Benefits Not Products

Boomers don't get emotional about products; we get emotional about the benefits the products provide. That's the key to selling to us: breaking down our sales resistance by talking about and demonstrating benefits, and helping us develop an affinity for the *experience* your solution provides. We want textures and materials that make us feel luxurious and comfortable, travel that makes us feel special and not part of a cattle drive. Service that makes us feel cared for and listened to, and home appliances and accessories that make us feel wealthier than we are.

— *Boomer Selling Insight* —
The difference between premium
products isn't logical, it's emotional

Take something we all have in our homes: the kitchen faucet. This simple water control device ranges in price from under $50 to over $1,000. What is the difference between a $50 faucet and a $1,000 faucet? Not much, really. The function is pretty much the same. The water pouring from both will be the same temperature, same purity and same pressure. It's highly doubtful the $1,000 faucet will last 20 times longer than the $50 faucet. We don't buy it because we need it, we buy it because we desire it. We're willing to pay more for a top-of-the-line faucet with a daring design and gleaming brushed nickel finish, not because we think it will give us better water, but because of the emotional benefits—a more affluent feel for our kitchen, a better feeling about where we are in life, maybe even envy from our friends. Appeal to our emotions. An example:

Product feature:	*Kitchen sink handle*
Logical benefit:	*Turns water on/off*
Emotional benefit:	*The stylish design and unique hand-rubbed finish will impress my friends and make me feel I've finally made it!*

As you can see, logic does play a role in all of this. Emotional benefits emerge from product features that offer a balance between logical, practical usefulness and sensual, emotional qualities. It works like this:

- Stage 1: Boomer encounters a kitchen faucet with features that include a premium finish and life-time warranty

- Stage 2: Boomer finds that the logical appeal of the life-time warranty and its reduction of risk supports the emotional appeal of the faucet's finish and design

- Stage 3: The sales consultant highlights both logical and emotional qualities until the customer's desire overcomes price objections and the sale is made

When we can afford it, Boomers will almost always buy the solution that offers the most emotional satisfaction, as long as we can convince ourselves that the logical features make the emotional purchase acceptable to ourselves and others. The higher our emotions are, the less we want to compare, the less important the price and the quicker we buy. When we want it, we want it and we want it now. If you as the consultant can fire up our emotions, you're going to make a lot more profitable sales. It's just that easy.

How Younger Consultants Lose Boomer Sales

The reason many younger sales consultants often lose out on Boomer sales has little to do with the generational divide, but with the fact that they try to sell the same way *they* buy. Gen X and Gen Y consultants came of age with the Internet, so they are very comfortable researching a product to a fare-thee-well before they buy. Many walk into a store armed with reviews from Epinions.com and ratings from Consumer Reports and know more about the MP3 player they want to buy than the consultant does. This isn't to say they aren't also emotional shoppers, because everyone is. But many younger buyers are as driven by a "Give me enough facts and I'll make a decision" attitude as by raw desire.

This approach doesn't work for Boomers and it's why younger consultants can make Boomers feel "oversold." We didn't come of age online and we're not fact-centric in our shopping. We trust our experience, which has served us well for so many years. We're a little like Lucy Ricardo in *I Love Lucy*, getting ourselves into one bizarre fix after another by trusting our instincts to guide us and ending up pretending to be the Maharincess of Franistan while Ricky and Fred gin up a fake assassination plot to scare us into being good. But we're never going to be good; and unless we're in the analytical minority, we're never going to walk into a company that builds swimming pools with a sheaf of notes about filtration ratios and the merits of chlorine versus ozone. It's not our style.

— *Boomer Selling Insight* —
You can't "reason" Boomers
into buying emotional products

Because our emotions play a much larger role in deci-sion-making during mid-life and later than they do in early adults, we need you to provide us with the right combination of rational and emotional information—*then please back off and let us sell ourselves.* This is where so many younger con-sultants shoot themselves in their Skechers. Our emotional involvement, not a laundry list of facts, is what determines if we buy and what we buy and who we buy it from.

Know Our Emotions and Bring Yours

If you want an easier selling experience and bigger commission checks, dog-ear this checklist:

- Boomers are less logically and rationally driven
- Boomers trust their emotions because of past buying experience
- Boomers resist rational absolutes and hyperbole
- Boomers are concerned with how their contem-poraries will view their purchase
- Boomers process emotional information more deeply and remember it longer than non-emo-tional information

We also expect you to bring some emotion to the sales process. Because first impressions are emotionally based, the boomer buying process starts the moment we first set eyes on a sales consultant. If we form a negative opinion about a consultant, it's much harder for us to reverse our feelings and get emotionally involved.

— Boomer Selling Insight —
Our level of enthusiasm will never be higher than yours

One of the biggest reasons Boomers don't buy someone's premium, customized solution isn't lack of money, but lack of interest and excitement. You should be able to be excited about what you're selling. The more we have to listen to a monotone voice droning out uninteresting features, facts, and figures, the less we're going to listen and the less likely we are to buy. If you're not fired up by what you're selling, we won't get fired up about buying. You can get us both revved-up and emotionally charged simply by using enthusiastic phrases like:

"This is exciting…"

"You're going to love this…"

"This is one of my favorite parts…"

It's no coincidence that the last four letters in enthusiasm is the acronym for "I Am Sold Myself."

We usually know what we want; we just want you to make it okay for us to buy it and to help us figure out which option is best for our lifestyle. You need to be listening to us and paying attention to the many cues that will tell you what rings our emotional chimes.

If you've been taking good notes during your initial consultation, you'll know our most pressing wants, needs and desires. You can turn a ho-hum sales presentation into an emotionally stimulating conversation with friends when you continue to talk about what's important to us:

1. Start each new topic by telling us how what you're going to say ties into *what* we told you we want. ("You said one of your goals is to…")

2. When presenting benefits, take time to bridge the gap between what we told you we want to *how* each benefit provides it. ("Here's how you'll get the reliability you're looking for…")

Many times the small act of tying what we want to what you're selling is the tipping point of the entire sale.

It's Kind of Like…

Metaphors (and similes, saying something is "like" something else) are another great way to bypass our pesky rational brain and get right to the gut. The less we need to think about what we're buying, the more likely we are to buy. The more familiar our mental image of what we're buying, the faster that new information becomes familiar and complex details understandable.

Metaphors also have a unique ability to forge a link from our unconscious thoughts to our conscious awareness. This is where you create the big "Ah ha!" moment that leads to the big sale. If you don't think

> **Metaphors build a bridge between what we know and what you're selling**

metaphors work, consider this: America went to war in Vietnam because of "the *domino effect* of spreading communism." Examples of effective metaphors and similes:

- "This car has the feeling that you got from the GTO you said you drove in high school"

- "Do you remember the feeling you had when you finally got your first bike? This can give you the same type of excitement"

- "You'll get the same feeling as a warm sweater on a cool night"

- "The annual energy savings from these windows could just about pay for an annual Caribbean cruise"

Our brains have an insatiable desire to produce good feelings. The better we feel, the more we buy. The next time you buy groceries, stop and listen. Chances are some of your favorite songs (or at least Boomers' favorites) are being played on the PA system. As you unconsciously flash back to a happy time, you're more likely to unconsciously grab two (high margin) filet mignons that weren't on your shopping list. Your subconscious mind is linking the song to the good time you had grilling steaks on the lake with friends while listening to the same song. It's all about emotions, baby!

Boomers have decades of strong emotions lying dormant just waiting for you to stimulate them with memories from our younger years. For instance, many of us came of age in the 1970s, when an oil embargo led to high gas prices and long lines at gas stations. For many Boomers, that was a powerful and uneasy time. If you're selling hybrid cars, talk about the days signs read "No Gas," and how ironic it was that we were going crazy over gas selling for 75 cents a gallon when we've paid over $4. We remember the anxiety we felt back then, and it's your ally when you're trying to get us to sign off on a loaded $30,000 Prius.

We Need to Understand

Comfort with a purchase is also an emotion, and we must have comfort that we're making a good choice. When we're faced with purchasing something complex, uncomfortable or new, Boomers can quickly go into a defensive mode where we:

- Don't buy

- Wait

- Gather more information.

When "gather more information" wins, we instantly start searching our mental storage system for data to help us make the right decision. The older we get the easier this is, because we have more years of data etched on our emotional hard drives. If we find the right information, it immediately passes from our subconscious storage system into a file labeled "reasons to buy." If we don't find the right information in a reasonably short period of time, the data search stops and the sale ends. We both can save a lot of time and aggravation if you use these tools to help us cultivate an understanding for what you're selling.

- **Tell a story about a past client you helped.** Unlike features, facts and figures, stories connect emotionally. Throughout history, stories have been one of the most powerful ways to build rapport, create understanding and get people emotionally involved. Because Boomers are more skeptical than younger buyers, stories are more important to us. A good story reduces our resistance by allowing us to draw our own conclusions. Stories give us the ability to remember key points and critical information, and as some of our memories get a little fuzzier with age, this matters. One of the most important things a story does is allow us to see ourselves using the product, experiencing good feelings and even being complimented by others. That's powerful stuff.

— *Boomer Selling Insight* —
Properly planned and well-structured
stories ignite Boomers' emotions

Stories also allow you to reveal past accomplishments without bragging, provide potentially boring facts in an interesting manner, set you apart from your competition, and sell more premium customized solutions. Third party stories give you a safe way to mention past mistakes and triumphs and provide non-threatening ways to warn us about the potential risks of not buying.

- **Help us get a visual sense.** We think in pictures, not words. The book is usually better than the movie because we use the theatre of the mind to create pictures no director could ever match. This can be your ally in selling. During the sales process, our subconscious mind is trying to visualize us using the product. Because buying is a series of decisions, once we see ourselves using the product and enjoying the experience, the most important decision has been made. The rest is just working out the details. You can supercharge this process by helping us get a mental, visual sense of:

- Good feeling and future happiness
- Personal comfort
- Loved ones
- Using it, enjoying it, and being complimented by others
- Beauty or style in the setting where the product is used
- Our own bodies and style
- Doing something we couldn't do before

After 24 hours, most Boomer buyers only remember one out of five benefits when you mention them only once, but after we see something in person or in a brochure our "benefit retention" more than *doubles*. Eighty percent of the information we gain comes through our eyes, so it's no wonder the time it takes to learn a new concept decreases by over 40% when we can see what we're considering rather than just hearing a description. Visuals also get us much more excited and motivated than words alone. It's much easier to get excited about owning it after seeing it.

Seeing is believing.

- **Slow down.** Too many consultants speak at "70 mph with gusts up to 140." The great sportscasters that we grew up with, like Mel Allen and Jack Brickhouse, had a slow, relaxed cadence that allowed us to follow the action. "Speed talking" makes us nervous. As we age, our hearing changes and we become less able to filter out background noise. Our brains don't really slow down, recent research has shown, but we have a harder time sifting through our minds for information because there's so much in there already after 40 plus years of living. Thus, one of the most overlooked opportunities you have as a consultant to set yourself apart from your competition is to match the tempo of your sales process to the speed of the Boomer buying process. In other words, slow down and don't be in such a rush.

> There have been more words added to the dictionary during the Boomer generation than any other time in history, including "comb-over," "heart-healthy" and "primary care"

The single best way to do this is to look us in the eye, enunciate every syllable in every word, and take a breath at the end of every sentence. If you're not doing this, I promise you'll be amazed at the results.

- ### It's All in the Words

    *"If you wish to persuade me, you must speak
    my words, think my thoughts, feel my feelings."*
    — *Cicero*

The spoken word goes right to the emotional center of our brain. Humans are verbal, language-based beings. Certain words (let's call them *emotional* words) trigger emotional reactions, which send messages to the mind and start us thinking about acquiring something to satisfy our emotional needs. Emotional words are like electrical switches in a complex circuit leading to the sale. Every time a switch closes, we're one step closer to a sale. Some examples:

- "With its proven reliability there's no need to be *apprehensive* when you need it most"
- "There's a special *peace of mind* knowing you're safeguarding the health of your entire family"
- "This is one way to *protect* the furniture your grandmother brought from the old country"

- "The attractive design and professional appearance can make you *proud* when your friends arrive"

- "We've never had a customer *regret* buying the best they could afford"

The most powerful words may be phrased as questions. Say you're a consultant in a kitchen and bath showroom. Here are some emotionally-based questions you could ask to build desire and move the buyer to the right level of customization:

- "What statement would you like the kitchen to make?"

- "What feelings would you like your guests to experience?"

- "How long have you been dreaming about your new home?"

- "What would you like the guest bath to say about you?"

- "How do you want it to feel?"

Just imagine eating every meal without any spices, no salt, pepper, garlic powder or Tabasco. Nada, zip, nothing. Emotional phrases are like the right spices in a great bowl of chili. Test drive some of these blue plate specials:

- Enhance protection
- Avoid frustration
- Save time
- Reduce stress
- Avoid embarrassment
- Don't be angry with yourself
- Avoid annoyance
- Relieve boredom
- Satisfy curiosity
- Enjoy health
- Reduce fear
- Gain knowledge
- Protect your income
- Eliminate guilt
- Avoid effort
- Take pride in
- Be self-reliant
- Eliminate surprises
- Take advantage of

- **Offer us more information based on our feed-back.** Boomer buyers start with different levels of experience, and that means becoming an expert at reading our level of knowledge in seconds by listening to what we're saying (and not saying) by asking "checking questions." If you give too much information to a customer who's a novice, you can lose the customer. If you give too little information to someone who's taken the time to educate themselves, you're similarly doomed.

The solution is to provide basic information, followed by, "Would you like to hear more about..?" If we don't want to know more about that aspect of your solution, move on. Give us the foundation of your next point and ask another similar question. Examples:

"Would you like me to elaborate?"

"Is there anything else I can cover?"

"Do you have any questions so far?"

This amazingly simple process puts Boomers at ease by putting us in control of the amount and flow of information we receive. Others to have in your repertoire:

- "Can you see how that will benefit you?"

- "How does that make you feel?"

- "Do you think that will give you what you're looking for?"

When you make "checking questions" your North Star and compass, you'll give buyers the opportunity to stop and think about what is really important and how comfortable we are with the process so far. By continually asking for our thoughts, you'll build a much stronger rapport and gain an amazing amount of invaluable information.

The Big Three

Boomers rarely have enough money to buy the best of everything or everything we want. Every buying decision comes down to a choice that's determined by three things:

1. How well you'll solve our problems
2. How good you make us feel
3. How many emotional benefits you provide

When you master the art of elevating our emotions, we will spend less money in other areas so we can afford to buy from you. Eventually, knowing we're going to be working with you will spark emotional triggers of trust and anticipation which will bring us back again and will make it fun to tell our friends.

Which words elevate emotions?

- Style
- Safety
- Status
- Health
- Beauty
- Savings
- Service
- Quality
- Comfort
- Prestige
- Pleasure
- Security
- Protection

- Innovation
- Acceptance
- Admiration
- Knowledge
- Recognition
- Convenience
- Appreciation
- Relationship
- Dependability
- Peace of Mind
- Reduced Stress
- Personal Growth
- Affordable Luxury

SIX

Boomers will buy when value outweighs price.

Validate Value

Karsten Solheim, inventor of the Ping putter, told a story about managing a shoe repair store during the Great Depression. When his nearest competitor lowered the price of new heels to 15 cents, Solheim placed a big sign in the front window announcing the same lower price. He said, "The first customer that came in asked me, 'Are the heels as good as they used to be?' Of course, I had to say 'Yes.' When the next two customers asked almost the same question, I realized by lowering the price people thought we had lowered the value. I took my sign down and resumed charging 25 cents for heels. It didn't take long to discover even during hard times, most people are more interested in a good value than a low price."

This is one lesson that Boomers learned from our Depression-era parents and grandparents that helps mold our buying behavior today. Boomers buy emotionally, but we won't write the check until we validate our decision by determining that we're getting the best value for our money. How do we define value? It varies with each person, which is why this may be the most challenging aspect of the Boomer Selling process.

Take cars. Some of us will buy a new car because it makes us feel better, look younger and shows the world how much money we have, especially if we're a man in our early fifties and the car in question is a convertible BMW roadster. We'll spend big bucks on seldom-used but ego-enhancing options. We know we'll lose thousands in resale value the second we buy it, and we'll probably owe more than it's worth when we sell it in two or three years for the next greatest thing, but we've got to have it now because it *fits our style*. All we need is a justification for our desire, and that could be anything from safety to reliability to better gas mileage. Add that all together and you get the Boomer Value Equation:

Emotional satisfaction +
Says something desirable about us +
Practical justification +
The sense that we're getting more than we paid for
= VALUE

The Eight Elements of Value

Many Boomers have fond memories of those old, scratchy, pink-tinted educational films they used to show in chemistry class when we were in school. The kind hosted by an über-geek in a short sleeve shirt, tie and crew cut, with a title like, "The Periodic Table...And You"? The teacher would thread the film (yes, film) through the reels of the projector, swearing under his breath, and then run the film for ten minutes until it broke and he had to summon the audiovisual guy, who would splice the ends together with tape. Ah, the good old days of education. Anyway, the films would walk us through some dreadfully dull lecture about helium or boron and how vital it was to modern life, blah, blah, blah.

Well, if you were in a Boomer Selling sales course and saw that kind of film, it would feature the Eight Elements of Value, *except* this time the excitement would be so electrifying you'd be sitting on the edge of your seat, because instead of talking about some abstract concept you may never use (when was the last time you were asked to quote the Periodic Table?), you'd be learning the secrets to sales success, prosperity and financial freedom. The Eight Elements of Value are:

1. People
2. Process
3. Product
4. Partners
5. Protection
6. Profits

7. Proposal

8. Price

1. People

"You're only as good as the people you hire"
– Ray Kroc, founder, McDonald's

Boomers not only "buy" the person selling the product, we must also be comfortable with everyone we meet along the way. During each sale, it's the consultant's responsibility to get us excited about the people who'll be supporting the product and us. Boomers want to know that everyone involved is trustworthy, knows what they're doing and are going to do it exactly the way we were told they would. We might want to know if your firm runs criminal background checks on its people. We might ask if your employee drug tests are graded on a curve (we came of age when Timothy Leary was telling everyone to "tune in, turn on and drop out," so we know a little about drugs and the havoc they can create).

Bolster our confidence. Mention your team's qualifications, training, skills and attitudes. Everyone who has any customer contact influences our perception of your value, level of satisfaction and the likelihood of future business and referrals. Tell us why you're safe to hire… but beware of over-promising. Don't tell us that your delivery crews are always on time, because then you've created in us the expectation that they'll be there before the clock ticks over to 9:01, and if they're not, we're going to be mad. Be reassuring but realistic. We can take it.

2. Process

"94% of all failure is caused by process, not people"
– Dr. W. Edwards Deming

The type of buyer you want to do business with will determine the type of sales process you use. If you're selling bottom-tier goods to entry-level buyers, your sales process is simple: *always have the lowest prices.* If you want to sell premium products to Boomer buyers, match your selling process to our buying process by validating value without using old-school manipulation, high pressure or phony games.

— Boomer Selling Insight —
Boomers with money made it by sticking to a process

We will feel much more comfortable being part of an efficient, informational, buyer-focused sales process that makes us feel you and your organization are caring practiced professionals.

Boomers also want to know about your "implementation process." Tell us how the project will be organized, delivered, set up, and so on. Answer likely questions before they arise: what time you will start; how long the work will take; how will quality be controlled? In the unlikely event there is trouble, tell us who we'll call and what to expect. Value can only be validated after our fears are eliminated. Knowing that there is a process in place to address 99% of possibilities makes us feel secure.

For example, when we were growing up, the kitchen was strictly the woman's domain. Mrs. Cleaver made roasts there, and ridiculous magazine ads featured heels-and-pearls-clad homemakers extolling the incredible, orgasmic virtues of the latest refrigerator. That was then. Now, the kitchen is the center of home life, and companies have sprung up to address Boomers' demand for premium gourmet kitchens with granite counters, track lighting, roll out shelves and so on. The best of these companies have a time-tested process for handling everything from estimates to change orders to angry husbands to backorders. Nothing is left to chance. That's what we expect.

3. Product

"There's hardly anything in the world that some fool can't make a little worse or sell a little cheaper."
– *John Ruskin*

Most Boomers reach a point in our lives where we are willing to trade money for more time, lower risk, reduced hassle, better quality of life and more peace of mind. After all, we've spent decades earning our money and, especially when we're approaching retirement, we feel that we bloody well *deserve* to have the good life. This sense of entitlement is your friend when you're in sales. We are not the Wal-Mart generation, even if we used to be. We want the best we can afford...and maybe a little beyond what we can afford.

When making any important purchase, we will typically choose to work with the sales consultant who does the best job of customizing the trade-up solution that best satisfies our unique wants, needs and desires. Over the years of making poor choices and paying too little, then living to regret it, Boomers finally realize at about age 40 or so that it's almost impossible to receive the benefits we want from entry-level, core-solution products. We went cheap in the past and regretted it, and we've spent 10 years working ourselves into a self-righteous lather over the idea that we've darned well earned the right to the best. The fact is, when given the opportunity over 80% of Boomers will pay more for the products that make us feel physically and emotionally better. Three of the most important reasons that most Boomers will choose premium products:

1. Our Depression-era grandparents and war-rationed parents taught us, "Buy quality and you'll pay once, buy cheap and pay twice."

2. Life has taught us, "We'll never get more than we pay for."

3. One day we realize, "We've never gotten mad at ourselves for buying the best."

4. Partners

"Treat your customers like lifetime partners."
— Michael Leboeuf

The strength of any chain is determined by its weakest link. Imagine value as links on a chain connecting a railroad car carrying gold bars (profits) to a powerful locomotive (sales). If any link in the chain is missing, your gold won't move. If a link breaks during the journey, your gold is left behind. One of the most overlooked links in your value chain is the people and companies who sell premium products to you. You can't pass the highest

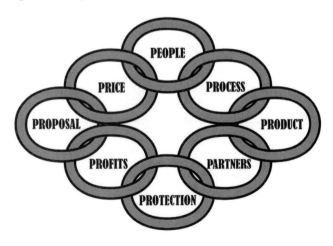

value down to your customers if your suppliers don't pass it down to you before, during and after every sale. Having the right products delivered, undamaged, to the right place, with the right paperwork, at the right time, with the right parts, pieces and accessories is invaluable!

Most Boomers don't care who your partners are or what challenges you face in dealing with them. That's not our problem and you're not going to get a drop of sympathy from us if something you promised doesn't happen because a partner dropped the ball. We see you as the captain of the ship: if a cabin steward forgets to close a porthole and our cabin floods, it's your fault. So it's vital that, behind the scenes, you make sure your partners are in line and delivering on what they promise, so you can deliver on your promises. If they can't deliver, replace them.

Example: A travel agency that specialized in selling luxury cruise packages to Boomers was losing referral business because of a bad link in its service chain. At an average price of about $12,000 per person, its cruises were so expensive that 70% of the company's new business came from satisfied customers telling their affluent friends about the fully-pampered experiences, but the shuttle company that ferried customers from their various airports to the departure docks had changed ownership and gotten sloppy and rude. The cruises were still wonderful, but the shuttle experience was unpleasant enough that it soured customers on the travel agency, even though they were not directly at fault.

The travel agency realized that every part of the travel chain—from booking to ticketing, to shuttle to the ship, to on-board service, to short excursions—had to be perfect, so they hired a host to ride every shuttle to assist guests and monitor their shuttle service experience. Within 12 months referrals had increased by over 10%.

5. Protection

Boomers know perceived risk is higher than the actual risk, but we wouldn't be caught dead without life insurance.

Before we will be comfortable buying from you, you must give us a level of protection that surpasses our concerns, fears and perceived risks. It's amazing how many sales are lost because consultants don't get credit for all the protection their company provides. The three rarely mentioned pillars of Boomer protection are *business licensure, insurance* and *warranties.*

Yes, there are far too many fly-by-night businesses named Cash. "Uh… just make the check out to "Cash." These dishonest shysters know any type of business license would alert the feds to their unethical (and illegal) business practices. Every Boomer has learned the hard way, if they'll cheat the government they'll cheat us. Once again, the most important thing Boomers shop for are people we can trust. If you make us nervous in this way, kiss any sale goodbye.

As we get older we become more risk averse. Your insurance also creates a cushion of fiduciary responsibility and, dare I say, legal comfort for us. Liability and workman's compensation insurance let us know that if our great-grandmother's clock gets broken or one of your workers gets injured on the job, we won't end up on the wrong side of the bench facing Judge Judy.

Warranties are like big fluffy blankets of protection and guaranteed potential cost savings for us. Odds are we won't need the warranty, but how often has a customer reacted with delight when they found out from you that a repair or replacement they assumed was going to cost them big was covered by their warranty? Warranties give us one less thing to worry about, and we need that.

6. Profits

> *"If you mean to profit, learn to please."*
> — *Winston Churchill*

Will your customized solution increase our gas mileage, reduce our water or electric bills, cut the lawn faster, extend the life of our clothes, or keep our food fresher? Even better, can you help us legitimately reduce the money we spend on taxes? If so, you have another amazing opportunity to use two of our favorite subjects to help us *justify* buying now. The fact is, we love money and are afraid of running out of it. If you can show us how what you're selling will help us save it or keep more of it, you've got our full and immediate attention. If you can do that while also reducing our tax bill, we may put you in our wills.

Here's an example of what I'm talking about in investment terms. Let's say your energy-efficient washing machine costs $1,000 and saves us $50 every year in reduced electric, water heating and water usage bills. That's a 5% return on investment, better than many retirement-bound Boomers have averaged over the life of our savings accounts. What's more, a dollar saved is better than a dollar earned because we don't have to pay taxes on it. Just the thought of legally avoiding taxes makes us salivate like Pavlov's little doggie.

And if you're selling something that can provide us with a tax credit, such as a high efficiency heating and air condition system, energy-efficient windows or solar panels, you're in like Flynn. We love getting The Man to pay for some of our purchases. So, if you haven't yet done the research into possible ways your customers can get a rebate from their utility company or save money on federal, state or local taxes by buying what you have to offer, now would be the time.

In fact, it's not a bad idea to have a printed sheet ready to hand to customers, with a breakdown of how your solution can save Boomers money and tax liability. Have a PDF version available to e-mail us as well. It could be the difference between a homerun and a strikeout.

7. Proposal

"The large print giveth and the small print taketh away."

— Unknown

The Boomer motto is "Don't tell me, show me." Or as Reagan said when the Cold War was still going strong, "Trust but verify." We learned that when we were almost turned into a smoking, glowing hole in the ground during the Cuban Missile Crisis. Even though we trust you, we still want what we talked about in writing. Think of your "proposal" (ever since *the Godfather* the word "contract" kind of scares us) as a partnership agreement that focuses on our needs, not yours. It should summarize the details for your entire customized solution and make clear how we'll get everything we told you we want. Everything we care about should be laid out as precisely as possible:

- Total cost (investment)
- Payment schedule (if any)
- Detailed description of the solution to be provided
- Delivery date

- Guarantees or warranties
- All contact information

Most consultants make the mistake of rushing this part of the process; don't do it. Before writing your proposal, remember, everything you write either adds or subtracts value, so mentally put yourself in your buyer's place. Ask yourself how logistical problems will be eliminated, how emotional concerns will be addressed. How will you protect the buyer's home, furnishings and family? How will you make your customers' lives safer, easier and less stressful? And don't forget to eliminate surprises by telling us what's *not* included.

Even if you have the kind of penmanship your eighth grade English teacher loved, don't hand write your proposal. Have a professional-looking Boomer-friendly proposal with print large enough to be read with Boomer eyes that are less than 20/20.

Whenever possible, don't e-mail, snail mail or fax your proposal to us. There usually are some questions that come up that we'd prefer to discuss with you in person. One of the many reasons to sell premium customized solutions instead of entry level products is you can afford to spend the face-to-face time some Boomers are going to need before we'll buy. All things being equal, the most detailed proposal validates the most value, and value is the key to Boomer Selling.

8. Price

"Where quality is the thing sought after, the thing of supreme quality is cheap, whatever the price one has to pay for it."

— *William James*

As the first Boomers approached middle-age, the world experienced runaway inflation. The French government tried to determine the cause of inflation by cutting cheeses in equal halves, then selling one half for 36 centimes and the other half for 56 centimes. The higher priced cheeses sold almost twice as fast. Why..?

Low prices create suspicion. We instantly wonder why we're paying less. Some people shop only on price, but they are usually lower-income individuals or folks who don't think about quality and value until something fails. Boomers are different. We've been around the block a few times which causes us to wonder. Have substandard safety components been used to build my chain saw? How many corners were cut? If I buy this, will I be supporting sweatshop labor? How many hidden costs will be added to the final price? Yes, it's not uncommon for once-burned, twice-shy Boomers to disqualify a business if their price is too *low*. Price as much as anything, is a symbolic indicator of value. Boomers know we usually get what we pay for.

Today, Boomers still use price as an indicator of quality and value. We know:

- A bargain isn't about what we pay, but what we receive
- We've come to believe that quality is never an extravagance
- We know the only free cheese is in the mousetrap

Every Boomer has paid too little for something important like accounting services, a construction bid, or auto repair and lived to regret it. We've learned the hard way that the "low bidder" is the one who left out something that we're going to need—and pay dearly for—later.

— Boomer Selling Insight —
We've discovered that if we pay less, we get
less, so intuitively we expect a customized
solution that includes more to cost more

We've learned that the total cost of a solution includes the time, effort and inconvenience of having to shop around, start the process all over, enlighten a new, unknown consultant, and maybe waste a great deal of effort being frustrated. In a way, we're your perfect customers.

The process we Boomers use to validate our decision to partner with you is like weighing gold on a balance beam scale. Price weights down one side while nuggets of value are added to the other. The second value out-weighs price, we start reaching for our credit card.

Value Not Validated Doesn't Exist

You may think what you are offering has value, but what really matters is how we, your Boomer customers, view every element in your entire package. If we perceive enough value to tip our mental scale, you're set. If not, you need to keep piling on the value or you can kiss us goodbye. Some key principles to follow:

- **Sales are won by grams, not pounds.** In today's volatile and uncertain economy, there is no such thing as a "big win." When dealing with customers, little things are vital, attention to detail is critical and everything you say or do adds or subtracts value. Remember, confidence is like fine crystal: hard to manufacture and easy to break. Small things like the speed of returned calls, met or unmet deadlines and the demeanor of delivery personnel can make or break business today and future business tomorrow.

- **Don't sell what it is, sell what it will do.** After you've determined what we want, tell us exactly what you can do. Avoid becoming bogged down in technical details and jargon. Instead, explain how the most important technical qualities and features provide the desired results. Talk about performance and effect on our lifestyle, health, comfort, safety, or whatever area of life your solution covers. Most Boomers don't want to know how the pulleys in the home gym you're selling work; he wants to know how fast he can look like the 97 pound weakling who cold-cocks the bully on the beach in the Charles Atlas "Made a Man out of Mac" ads on the backs of old comic books.

— Boomer Selling Insight —
Benefits must be proven, not just listed

- **Focus on long-term benefits, not short-term savings.** When it comes to spending money, most people think about the immediate impact of their purchase. But Boomers have learned that thinking short-term can have a disastrous effect when making major decisions. If you're looking out for *our* best interest, you have an obligation to help us think long-term. Show how each dollar spent today will pay huge financial and *emotional* dividends tomorrow. Help us visualize enjoying these benefits long into the future and tell us again why it's in our best interest to spend a little more right now. One of the biggest benefits in selling premium products with the Boomer Selling process is simple: Boomers won't have to endure the hassle of shopping for new appliances, carpeting or furniture again for many years if they buy the best from you now.

- **Boomers determine value by comparison, so compare.** Use brochures and sales literature to show pictures of the products and accessories that best meet our needs. Without knocking your competition show us side-by-side comparisons so we understand how much better your solution is. Explain how special features provide the benefits Boomers want most. Keep building value with phrases like:

  - "What this means to you is ..."
  - "Here's why that's so important..."
  - "This is one of the most important parts..."

Value comes mostly from benefits, so never hesitate to review everything that is important to us and show how true comparison is impossible.

- **Demand raises value, bidding lowers it.** To increase demand, you reduce supply. That's basic

Adam Smith economics. That's why I advise you not to get into situations where you're forced to bid against your competitors. When you offer unique benefits that your competitors have failed to provide, the demand for your offering increases. On the other hand, bids are almost always accepted based on the lowest price, and it is impossible to provide the greatest value for the lowest cost. Once again, when Boomers see that you offer the greatest value, most will be willing to pay more to deal with you.

— Boomer Selling Insight —
Until desire has been created, value doesn't matter

- **Don't confuse overpriced with under-desired.** Desire is a craving for something not yet obtained. To create desire, explain what's wrong with the present situation and show how you'll improve or correct it. Because desire grows with knowledge, provide hard evidence to reinforce the value of your offer. That really starts tipping our value scale in your favor.

- **To build more value, add more benefits.** Value, like quality, is what people say it is. What is valued by one Boomer buyer may be insignificant to another. Every customized solution offers dozens of benefits. But most Boomers will have an overwhelming interest in only three or four, and that's why determining our desires is so important to your sales success.

— Boomer Selling Insight —
Wrap your presentation around our desired benefits and don't hesitate to review them often

- **Reduce supply to a single source: you.** If you're not careful, most products can become commodities. Boomers can get water purification systems, garden tractors and landscaping services from many different sources. The unique thing that sets you apart is you and the people behind you—your level of knowledge and service, your commitment to satisfaction, your creativity in developing the perfect full-featured solution, your willingness to go the extra mile, your desire to have a long-term relationship. The cornerstone of value is trust. The more Boomers trust you, the more we will trust your company and solution, and the more value we will both receive. The more you customize your solution to solve our problems, the tighter you lock-out your competition and the more referral business we're going to give you.

- **Do things your competition won't...or can't.** When you extend benefits your competition doesn't offer, you create a special and unique kind of value. One benefit that can eliminate your competition and drive your value quotient into the stratosphere is *guaranteed peace of mind*. When customers know that whatever happens you'll take care of it, our resistance melts like a fudgsicle in July. That's why companies offering ultra-premium products like Mercedes-Benz offer warranties that cover everything, including routine maintenance. Such coverage conveys the subtle message that, "We understand you're too busy and successful to worry about such things, so we'll worry about them for you."

Unlike a power monopoly that's illegal under the Sherman Anti-trust Act, a Value Monopoly helps you and your customers be more profitable, and is totally legal

How to Create a Value Monopoly

Billionaire J. Paul Getty said, "If you want to make money, really big money, do what nobody else is doing." The way to make really big money is to create a *Value Monopoly*. We're not talking about the board game with Community Chest and Park Place, either. A monopoly is "the exclusive control that makes possible the fixing of prices and the virtual elimination of competition." You can cook up a Value Monopoly by mixing together the following ingredients:

- **Unmatched reliability.** Talk is cheap, but proven reliability is priceless. Half the auto manufacturers would be out of business if people didn't justify buying a new car because their old one is "unreliable". McDonalds became the world's leading fast food purveyor because of consistency, not because they have the best tasting burgers. When you go into a McDonalds in Prague, you know you're going to get a Big Mac that tastes the same as one bought in Evanston, IL (and you know you'll always find a clean bathroom, which is a godsend when you're traveling).

— Boomer Selling Insight —
Reliability and consistency are the
most neglected sources of value

Ways to demonstrate reliability include testimonial letters that document specific instances of reliability, showing customers the crossed-out names of former competitors in a four-year-old phone book, and showing in-house reports that demonstrate average emergency response time or turn-around time.

- **Unrivaled response time**. The easiest way to cancel out value is to be slow to respond when a customer has a problem. The opposite is also true. We're all accustomed to being kept waiting by monolithic corporations that don't care about our business, so when you can respond on a dime, we will love you. One of the biggest reasons Dominos has become the biggest pizza chain in the country is because you always know you're going to get your hot pizza in 30 minutes, period. They're fast and responsive. You'll increase your value and customer base. The keys to rapid response are ongoing communication and anticipating customer needs. Have systems in place to enable you to respond quickly with what the customer needs.

- **Take responsibility**. Nothing makes us madder than when someone in a company passes the buck when there's trouble. We occasionally want someone to blame and bawl out and, if that's you, take a big gulp, swallow your pride and take it. When you do this, our stock in you climbs to a new high. But more often we just want to feel like someone is going to take charge of solving our problem.

— *Boomer Selling Insight* —
The profit you make is limited
by the responsibility you take

When you take full responsibility, you're allowed to receive full profits. Consider offering a guarantee of something like response time, quality or measureable return on investment, and make sure it's clear what the buyer gets if you don't meet your guarantee. When you guarantee results you eliminate competition, abolish risk, erase price resistance, and eliminate reasons why customers shouldn't buy now.

- **Base your price on value, not cost**. Boomers buy the value that comes out, not the price that goes in. If you want higher profits, your only choice is to provide higher value. When setting prices, understand all the benefits your customized solution provides and price appropriately.

- **Make value measureable**. If you don't quantify the value you can provide, your customers will be forced to base the price we're willing to pay on our *perception* of the value you offer—and in most cases, the assumed value is almost always less than the actual value you provide. For instance, the Toyota Prius, the runaway bestseller among high-mileage cars, is a mega-hit because dealers can easily quantify its main benefit: savings on gasoline. If they were just talking about the cool hybrid engine and the other high-tech features, they would still sell cars, but not as easily nor as many.

Customers don't know about the benefits of your manufacturing process, your service system or your computerized record keeping, so tell us. Reduced dollar costs are the easiest aspects of value to measure. When selling a product, analyze all possible costs during its life (maintenance, modification, supplies, depreciation, etc.) and show how you have the lowest total ownership cost. When selling a service, analyze how it reduces time, increases fun, or provides peace of mind. Whenever possible, use hard evidence to prove the value you're providing.

— Boomer Selling Insight —
Value not documented in the
Boomer's mind doesn't exist

- **Document your value.** To gain more new customers, document the value you will provide in your proposal. The more benefits you document, the more value you create. Whenever possible, detail how long-term savings will pay for costs, such as with a tankless water heater or home comfort system. Explain how fast the customer will receive the benefits. Show how the cost of prevention is much less than the cost of correction (a powerful statement of value). Reveal how you can manage the buyer's needs faster and better than anyone else. Show how certain the customer can be of receiving the value you offer by listing and reviewing everything you will do.

- **Measure satisfaction**. Boomer satisfaction is determined by the value we receive. One way to determine if the value you offer meets or exceeds the value we require is with a "value survey." A value survey measures your reliability, response, professionalism, reasons the customer bought from you instead of your competitor, etc. A phone call after a product is purchased or service is provided can help you determine the level of satisfaction your customer perceives they have received.

Sure, this process can be a bit nerve-wracking, like going in to take your SATs or final exams in college. You're on the spot and you're going to find out how well you performed. But if you don't find out, how will you know how you can improve?

- **Provide details**. Detail what the customer's current product or service is costing them. Use facts and figures to prove how much you can reduce or eliminate those costs with your customized solution. Try things like, "See, this is what your current washer/dryer combo is costing you per month in excess energy and water usage, versus what this high-efficiency, front-loading combo could save you." In this way, your proposal should also be a sort of investment prospectus. Detail how customers will receive more than they pay. Show them how they "can't live if living is without you."

- **Value trumps quality**. In the early 1900s, several companies produced extremely high quality buggy whips. But with the arrival of Ford's horseless carriage, their superior quality was worthless because their benefits weren't needed and buggy whip and harness companies went broke. Today, when Boomers buy any product we instinctively believe it will perform its designed function as promised. We take quality for granted; it's your cost of admission. To get our business, you have to provide the highest value; the highest quality is already assumed.

- **Follow up**. Follow up is your secret weapon. Following up promptly and thoroughly can bury the competition by assuring the customer that they are getting everything you promised and more. Following up can also reveal problems before the customers know about them, allow you to build a stronger bond with customers, and provide an opportunity to ask for referrals and receive additional business. Get on the phone and make calls; don't rely on e-mail or other impersonal methods. Talk to your customers, and instead of trying to duck problems, relish them as chances to show just how good you really are.

A Value Monopoly not only changes the rules, it changes the game, and it's hard to lose when it's your game and you're the only one who knows how to play it.

Thomas Edison discovers value

In 1870, Western Union owned a stock printer that had a series of problems. The "ticker" worked fine for a while, but then it would start running wild and printing crazy figures. Thomas Edison was hired to solve the problems and in short order had eliminated Western Union's costly downtime. He then met with a group of company directors who were profoundly impressed with Edison's work and the profits they would soon make with his improvements. One of the directors, General Lefferts asked, "Well young man, the committee would like to settle up your account, how much do you think it's worth?" Edison wanted $5,000 but knew he would settle for $3,000. Not sure how to answer, he said, "General, suppose you make me an offer." Lefferts replied without hesitation, "How would $40,000 dollars strike you?" The young inventor eagerly accepted. Like Edison's stock ticker, the value of your customized solution isn't determined by the price that goes in, but the value created by the benefits Boomer buyers receive.

SEVEN

When done correctly, the natural conclusion is, "I'll buy!"

Attain Agreement

After graduating from high school I had the opportunity to work on a crew fighting a huge forest fire on Bill Williams Mountain in northern Arizona. Besides the unlimited T-bone steaks and paper sleeping bags, the thing I remember most is a team of experts burning a huge area in front of the fire; when the fire hit the charred firebreak it stopped dead in its tracks because all the fuel was gone. It was amazing.

Using Boomer Selling is like building a firebreak for objections. If you've done everything according to the process up to this point, you've comfortably, systematically reduced the fuel that causes the vast majority of buyers to pull out of the sales process. The beautiful thing about Boomer Selling is that it eliminates the need for tricks, manipulation or pressure, while making you a more effective seller. But before Boomers will write out a check or throw our plastic on the counter, there's a darned good chance we'll try some tricks of our own. Don't underestimate the craftiness of a 50-year-old Boomer couple trying to save $300.

We Need to Prove Our Negotiating Kung Fu

Mark Twain must have been talking about Boomers when he said, "A man pretty much refuses another man's first offer, no matter what it is." I think what he meant was, "A *real* man or woman." That's black belt confrontation; and negotiation and deal-making have pretty much become the hand-to-hand combat of the Boomer age. We don't go at it with pistols at 20 paces like Alexander Hamilton and Aaron Burr, or throw down with a six-shooter in the dusty streets of a small western town like Gary Cooper in *High Noon*, so instead we parry over an $80 deliver charge and dodge a $250 extended service package.

Objections aren't brought up because we don't want to buy. Boomers can be ready, willing and able to buy but still throw objections at you like Ninja throwing stars. Why? Because we know the more time and energy a consultant has invested, the more *they* don't want to lose the sale. Many Boomers play on the fact that the consultant's potential loss of a big sale is not only financial but *emotional*. We've found that asking a question like "Is that the best you can do?" often leads to price cut or concession. We're like Dirty Harry in the famous "Do you feel lucky? Well, do ya, punk?" scene: we've just got to find out how many bullets you have in your gun. Sure, plenty of Boomers will throw out phony objections, not because we want to make the sale a little more contentious, but because we have nothing to lose and everything to gain. It's just that simple.

This is Boomer insight more powerful than Dirty Harry's .44 caliber revolver, "The most powerful handgun ever made:"

— Boomer Selling Insight —
After you take us through the Boomer Selling process, we are going to be convinced there is only one place to get you, your company and *our* customized solution

Yes, we may try to surgically remove some of your commission from your bank account, but if you don't fall for our straight-faced attempted commission-ectomy and stick to your guns—value, value, value—we'll almost always pay full price to get exactly what we want and be glad we did.

Old School Selling is Kryptonite for Commissions

During the Great Depression, there was a struggling country druggist who came up with a novel idea to earn extra money. He'd take the eggs his laying hens produced and sell them in his drug store. He quickly found folks didn't think much of buying eggs at a pharmacy. His store, like most at that time, had a soda fountain, so, he thought, why not ask customers if they wanted to add an egg to their malted milk for an extra nickel. After the first week he hadn't sold a single egg. So he thought, instead of asking people if they wanted an egg in their malted, he ask, "Do you want one egg or two?" By now you've guessed the happy ending. Not wanting to spend a dime, folks would say, "Just give me one egg." The druggist simply added five cents to the price of a malted and voila! Extra income.

According to urban legend, this was the first "alternative of choice close." This "Would Tuesday at 1:00 or Wednesday at 4:00 be best for you?" old-school sale maneuver may have worked on our parents and grandparents (even though the druggist probably didn't sell a lot of malted raw eggs), but in modern times, all these kinds of manipulative sales techniques do is leave us with a bad taste in our mouths. We've heard just about every memorized sales line in the book, dealt with all the high-pressure tactics and seen just about every trick there is. When a car salesman asks, "What do I have to do to sell you this car today?" we're likely to reply, "Give it to me for one dollar, you bozo."

Every time we encounter a manipulative, high-pressure sales approach, we associate it with some kind of bad product, bad feeling or bad deal. When our subconscious mind picks up on a shopworn selling strategy, it starts throwing up defensive maneuvers that would make Muhammad Ali proud. Why make us pull out our obnoxious salesperson kryptonite when you could take a different approach and be Superman (not the flabby 1950s George Reeves kind but the modern six-pack abs guy) for your bank account and your company?

Know Objections and Eliminate Them

The answer to this problem is not to bull your way through the sales process milepost-by-milepost, checking off steps and statements, without seeing how much steam is coming from our ears. It's to find out what our real objections are so that you can counter them and finally attain our agreement that the solution you're offering at the price you're offering is the best for us. But you can't do that until you know what our objections are. As hockey great Wayne Gretzky said, "You always miss 100 percent of the shots you never take."

In the late 1920s Henry Ford bought one of the largest life insurance policies in America. The policy was so large it was the subject of a front page story in the Detroit newspaper. A close friend who happened to sell life insurance called Ford and asked "Henry, you know I sell insurance, why didn't you buy that big policy from me?" Without hesitation, Ford said, "You never asked." *Ouch.*

— Boomer Selling Insight —

The best way to ask Boomers to buy is to imagine
we said, "We'll take it..." just tell us what to do next

As strange as it seems, many consultants never give Boomers an opportunity to buy

For a large percentage, "closing" is synonymous with trickery, which can be true with traditional high-pressure selling. At the other extreme, ethical consultants using a flawed sales process have a natural tendency to avoid asking potential clients to buy, because they are afraid they will come across as pushy, even distrustful. It's just not in their character. But the problem isn't so much asking for the order as it's having to deal with objections. To avoid pain, the untrained ethical seller's subconscious mind says, "If I don't ask them to buy, I won't have to use some uncomfortable tactic to deal with their objections." So they don't ask and the Boomer doesn't buy and everyone loses.

Simply said, you need to give us a chance to buy—ask for the sale, then step back and give us some room to come to agreement with you. One of the most comfortable ways to do this is to use your proposal as a sales closing tool.

— Boomer Selling Insight —
The greatest momentum is near the end of the
Boomer Selling process when you are going over
our proposal line-by-line, benefit-by-benefit

Every time you mention something we want, the value gets bigger and the price gets smaller. When we see detailed in writing everything we're getting, our excitement grows and the momentum becomes nearly unstoppable. This excitement keeps building as you move to the lines marked "price," "down payment," "terms," and "acceptance." At that line, simply say something like, "All I need is your okay here and we can get started."

Objection Extermination Made Simple

That said, don't be surprised if we don't jerk the pen out of your hand and immediately sign on the dotted line. Remember, we Boomers are strongly inclined to raise objections. That's just our nature. Please don't take it personally. Here's a deep secret we hate to admit and we'd rather you didn't know. *We're predictable.* In fact we're so predictable that over 90% of all Boomer objections can be neatly placed into four categories:

1. Price
2. Affordability

3. Hesitation

4. Comparison

Price. Be happy we're trying to knock you down on price. If we weren't interested in buying, price wouldn't be an issue. Just about every Boomer's favorite objection has something to do with price. Why? Boomers have learned that in any kind of negotiated sale (and we know that just about everything can be negotiated) if we say something like, "Your price is too high" and then shut up, the consultant is likely to add a little more to our pile of benefits at no additional cost.

The reason many consultants needlessly give benefits away (cutting into their own bottom line) is that they lack a process to deal with real objections and *Boomer manipulation.* Dealing with price objections is easier and a whole lot more rewarding than trying to figure out if Dirty Harry just fired six shots or only five. The process for neutralizing price objections:

a. Review the benefits.

This is powerful language: "To make sure I didn't include something you didn't want, why don't we review your priorities." That rocks us back on our heels. We were expecting you to grovel, and you didn't. Take out your notes and review everything we told you we want.

Briefly mention how your customized solution will take care of each item on your list. Wait for our acknowledgement; since it's really our list and our ideas we'll say something like, "That's right", or we'll nod our head, we'll give you some kind of feedback. If you come across something we told you we could probably live without, ask if we want it taken out. This usually stops us like a pachyderm in a tar pit.

— Boomer Selling Insight —
Every time you review the benefits
value gets bigger and the price gets smaller

When you offer to take something away, it's in our nature to want to keep it. The ball is now in our court and the only pressure is what we're putting on ourselves. After we do our mental gymnastics and still don't want some element in the package, remove it. Don't overlook the fact that every unwanted feature is a potential objection.

After reviewing everything on your list, remind us that … "The price reflects everything you were looking for."

> "We always give our best price up front"

b. Provide assurance

Almost every Boomer has a little bit of insecurity hiding under our confident demeanor. When we're buying big-ticket items, a little assurance goes a long way. In the late 1980s it seemed like everyone who could read a wiring schematic was making and selling personal computers. I needed to replace my old 8088 computer because the 20 megabyte hard drive's memory was almost full (I know, it's hard to believe in these days when skinny laptops routinely come with *gigabytes* of memory, but there were indeed times when computers had no drives, only 5 ¼" floppy discs).

I found a store and a full-time salesperson who showed me an amazingly fast computer called a 286. The only problem was it wouldn't work on the DOS operating system I had been using; it required a new program called Windows. I didn't want to learn a whole new program, then have to learn yet another one in a year or two when the next generation of computers came out. I kept asking the salesperson, "Am I doing the right thing?" "Are you sure I won't have to buy a new program next year called Doors and Siding?" "Am I doing the right thing?" The sales rep stopped, looked me in the eye and said, "Everyone will soon be using Windows; I guarantee you're making the right decision. You won't regret it." I was relieved; the sales consultant's assurance gave me the confidence I needed to buy. My only regret was not buying 1,000 shares of Microsoft stock the same day.

— *Boomer Selling Insight* —
Don't hesitate to reiterate

As much as we Boomers want to be in control of the buying process, most of us need a surprising amount of assurance before we'll make a major buying decision. Remind us again about the problems we're trying to solve, and the many ways your solution gets the job done, saves us money or makes our lives better. Give us confidence that we're being smart shoppers.

c. Offer to reduce benefits

Buyers with deep and real price concerns may tell you again that, "The price is still too high." At this point, way too many consultants would be tempted to cut their price to get the sale. But instead of making an instant sale, there's a good chance you'll make us instantly mad. Most Boomers will be thinking, "If you can cut your price now, why didn't you cut it in the beginning? How much too much are you still overcharging me? If you weren't honest with the price earlier how can I trust you now?" Bang. Dirty Harry just shot you between the eyes. If you make us feel that you've been playing games with us or jerking us around, or intentionally wasting our time, you'll end up wearing a dead sale toe tag.

Instead of cutting your price and opening a cage of rattlesnakes you may never get closed, give *us* the opportunity to cut the price by taking something out. Review your notes again, starting with *our* highest priorities, and discuss the pros and cons of removing or reducing each benefit. "One of your major concerns was quiet operation; we could go with another model that's not quite as quiet and the warranty is two years less than the *premium system*." Whoosh, the ball is back in our court again. Every time you review the benefits we want, the value gets bigger and the price gets smaller because we get one more chance to remind ourselves how much we really do want that benefit. If we didn't want it, we wouldn't have put it on the list in the first place, right?

> **We always resist losing things we want**

The more we want it the more we'll resist losing it. Don't be surprised if we start selling *you* on why we need to keep it all. If Boomers want what you're selling enough (remember the chapters on determining desires and elevating emotions) we'll find the money to buy it!

Affordability

This is different from price. Pricing is perceived as something that's in your control, but when Boomers cite affordability concerns, we're talking about our own financial comfort zone. Remember back in the *Determine Desires* and *Elevate Emotions* chapters how Boomers worry more about a potential loss of money than we savor a possible gain? Your affordability-centric Boomer client is like a contestant on *Let's Make a Deal* who has won the

Formica dining room set but is given an opportunity to choose one of two doors to win a new car, and decides to stick with the dining room set. Never mind that she has a 50/50 chance of winning a car; her focus is on not losing what she's got, even though if she picked the door with the push lawn mower behind it, she'd be no worse off than when she arrived at the studio.

When lack of money is a *real* problem, two great ways to make your solution more affordable are:

- Reduce the benefits—Even though we may desire your customized solution, not every Boomer can afford it as designed. When you help us reduce the benefits to lower the price to a level we can afford, we give up some things we wanted but still get a more than acceptable solution. We both still win. You have no idea how much we appreciate your help with making a compromise in a dignified way. We also appreciate your attitude of, "Whatever you choose to buy is the right thing to buy."

- Help us find the money—Boomers have 70% of the wealth in the U.S., and the vast majority of us made it by borrowing other people's money. Boomers are the most creditworthy people in our economy. Some of us have been living in the same house for years and still have a mountain of untapped home equity. Others have made financial mistakes in the past but have had time to recover. Many of us are going through some serious life changes. We've finally realized we're approaching the short half of our lives. If we don't tap our financial resources and splurge today, when will we?

Never hesitate to offer Boomers financing. Keep it simple. When it comes to repayment, give us the longest terms and the smallest payments possible. We've been around the block a time or two; if we don't want to finance or prefer a shorter term, we'll let you know. The more interest rate options (for less than perfect credit) and repayment terms your financing program has, the better. Also, if your customized solution saves us money that you can quantify, deduct those savings from the monthly payment to reduce our total out-of-pocket ownership cost.

Hesitation

You'll know this objection is in play when you hear the age-old phrase, "We need to think about it." The fact is some Boomers want to make an immediate decision and get it behind us. Others love to procrastinate, hoping maybe the thing they want will go on sale or they will come into their inheritance. Some Boomers really do need to think about it (especially if they grew up in a home where finances were really tight and they don't spend more than $100 without some major soul searching), while others get cold feet but don't want to admit it. In any case, you have no choice but to respect our desire to hesitate. The alternative is to disrespect us, and to paraphrase *The Godfather*, "Disrespect will leave you with nothing but a bullet-riddled ego and some cannoli."

Early in our marriage, Charlotte and I tried to buy a used car. We found one we liked and wanted to buy, but after a really bad buying experience with a door-to-door vacuum cleaner scam artist (those were the days before Truth in Lending laws), we made a pact that we'd never again rush into buying anything. We told the salesman we wanted to "sleep on it" and would come back the next day. The jerk said, "I've got a mattress in the back room; you can put it on top of your car and sleep on it, ha, ha, ha." If you guessed we bought another car from different dealership, you would be right.

Most Boomer couples make joint decisions when buying big ticket items. One of the most courteous and important things a consultant can do is give us a few minutes alone so we can go through our ritual: He turns to her and says, "What do you think?" She turns to him and says, "I don't know, what do you think?" We've learned the hard way if we don't both participate in this sacred ceremony and something goes wrong, one of us is going to hear about it for the life of the product. Find something you need to do for a few minutes. Go to the bathroom. Offer to get everyone some coffee. But whatever you do, don't go talk to your sales manager. That gives us the creeps.

— *Boomer Selling Insight* —
You cannot solve problems or deal with
objections you know nothing about

If, after you return, we still need to "think about it," ask, "Would you share your concerns with me?" This is like a doctor asking, "Where does it hurt?" If you've built the kind of rapport and confidence you should have created through the Boomer Selling process, then we should be ready (even glad) to tell you what the problem is in hopes you can solve it. It's wonderful how many times this question will help you find the real objection (which *almost* never has anything to do with "thinking about it.")

A word of caution. Some Boomers have a hard and fast rule that we think about our buying decision overnight or longer. The more expensive the purchase, the more wary we're going to be and the more leeway we need from you. Give these buyers all the time they need but before leaving, agree on a time, place and means of following up. You should always be the one to initiate the follow-up call or visit, not the buyer.

Comparison

This objection will most often be manifested in the phrase, "We need another bid" or "We can get the same thing cheaper somewhere else." That's translation for, "You blew it." The three most common reasons Boomers tell you they want another bid are:

1. You didn't ask the right questions

2. You failed to provide enough benefits to justify the price

3. You forgot to review the benefits

Boomers have grown up with folks like the talking-head consumer advocates on local news channels telling us we need to get three bids for everything. But when you follow the Boomer Selling process, it's *impossible* for your customer to make an "apples to apples" comparison between you and a competitor because no one else has the same apples. Period! Once again, the key here is *you*, not the product. Customers can't get your knowledge or your company's commitment to excellence anywhere else, and if you demonstrate that, you'll derail a great deal of comparison shopping.

You're offering something completely unique in terms of your expertise, service, knowledge, benefits and commitment to buyer satisfaction. So when buyers say they need to shop around, or they tell you they can get the same thing cheaper elsewhere, resist the temptation to say, "No, you can't." Say something like, "If you talk to others, there are three extremely important things to keep in mind...if you'd like, I'll jot them down for you." Take out a pad and pen and review every benefit that the buyer helped design into their solution. Briefly explain again how your customized solution is the only way to give them exactly what they want. Remind them of the benefits of doing business with your company, the value of your highly trained people, their dedication to quality, and their commitment to total customer satisfaction. Last, remind your Boomers of the most important thing they can't get anywhere else at any price: YOU. Let us know you'll be there for us, that you're job is to take any worries off our shoulders and put them on yours. After reviewing all your unique benefits, this is a great place to say, "With your OK, I'll take care of everything..." If you've followed the Boomer Selling process, a large number of Boomers will buy right then and there! For those who still want to shop around, no worries, you've armed us with a yardstick we'll use to measure others and a list of requirements that only you can fulfill.

Imagine you're the buyer...

Imagine you're looking for a company to do a complete kitchen remodel that you've been planning for years.

As you know, a lot of companies offer this service ranging from Big Box retailers to small family owned firms. You've collected brochures and got rough estimates from three possible vendors. Because of the way you were treated you really liked the consultant who worked for a small local company that specialized in kitchen and bathroom remodels, but because her proposal was the highest by almost 20% you said you wanted to shop around some more.

Now imagine the young sales consultant said;

- "I want to make sure you get the best job possible…., if you don't mind I'd like to write down some of the most important things for you to look for…"

- "One of your priorities was attention to detail. To assure each seam is almost invisible you may want to ask how the abutting edges of the granite will be smoothed, drawn together and held in place. Also, ask if a color pigment will be added to the sealant and if you can choose the color you want."

- "One very important questions to ask is if a Tyvek moisture barrier will be used between the granite and the decking, like we do, to eliminate rot and mold. Also ask if Latacrete 310 glue will be applied to join the granite to the decking. These two products are more expensive but can easily pay for themselves with longevity and peace of mind."

- "There are natural high and low spots on every piece of stone so if there are gaps between the granite and the decking, the countertop could crack over time. The key to keep this from happening is the shimming procedure. In fact the reason we can offer our 5 year "No-Crack" guarantee is the special shimming process we use."

- "This is very important; please make sure that one full piece of granite, like in our plan, will be used to cover your entire island. To save the cost of an extra slab it is not uncommon for two or more pieces of granite to be fitted together, but from what you said, I don't think you'd be happy with an unnecessary seam. It's also a common practice to charge $200 to $400 extra for the sink and plumbing cutouts that we've included in your proposal, so this is worth checking out."

- "It's a good idea to make sure all exposed granite will be treated with a full application of deep penetrating sealer. After that dries, each square inch of the surface should be polished to a smooth reflective finish. Just imagine how you'll feel when you first walk into your kitchen and see your beautiful new granite countertops shining back at you..."

Would you like me to make a list of the most important things to look for with your new cabinets...?"

Let's analyze what just happened. Because the consultant used the Boomer Selling process she had everything in place (without tricks, manipulation or pressure) to allow you to sell yourself.

Create Confidence

It was easy for the consultant to be honest and sincere when she said, "I want to make sure you get the best job possible..." because she had confidence you couldn't find the same value anywhere at any price. Confidence creates confidence.

Determine Desires

When the consultant reviewed one of your top priorities, did you get the feeling she had been listening and really cared?

Customize Solutions

The consultant mentioned often overlooked quality brands that are an important part of her customized solution.

Reduce Risk

The consultant explained how to avoid big problems with a procedure she knew her competition never mentions. Without knocking them, she explained how her competitor's procedures were not equal to hers. The frosting on the cake was the 5 year "No-Crack" guarantee.

> According to a survey commissioned by the National Association of Home Builders entitled, *Boomers on the Horizon – Housing Preferences of the 55+ Market,"* 77% of Boomers would buy a smaller home on a smaller lot and drive farther to work and shopping before they would scrimp on the quality of materials going into their homes

Elevate Emotions

When the consultant asked you to imagine your new kitchen with the sparkling new granite countertops, could you see them shining back at you? Could you feel the excitement? Did the price difference seem much less important by now?

Validate Value

The consultant validated value by detailing her superior procedures and better warranty. She poured on extra value by explaining there would be no extra costs or hidden surprises. She also reviewed the single most important element of value; getting exactly what you want.

Attain Agreement

If you truly wanted a quality kitchen remodel, would you buy from this consultant? If for some reason you still wanted to talk to other companies, would you use her list of recommendations and important things to look for? How many of her competitors do you think can win her game playing by her rules?

Attaining agreement is also about making your Boomer customers feel that they, not you, did the wheeling and dealing and showed their consumer chops. It's about putting us in the position to feel smart, feeling like we have the upper hand and can't be taken advantage of. It's about feeling like we've got the greatest value for our money. When you do this, you've put us in a place where we can comfortably say, "OK, let's do this thing."

When you master the Boomer Selling process, you'll be a wizard at making your Boomer customers feel cared for and respected, yet savvy and skilled at the art of the deal.

More to the point, you'll be like an experienced firefighter (or maybe Robert De Niro in *Backdraft*): knowledgeable and skilled and able to put out even the trickiest fire without it becoming an emergency. Objections will turn from wild fires to warming fires when you become a master at attaining our agreement by providing value we cannot match anywhere else.

The High Cost of a Low Price

When faced with a tough sale, it is not uncommon to find consultants who either start with a low price or cut their price during the sales process. When all the facts are in, no firm today can afford the high cost of a low price:

- **Current profits are reduced or eliminated**–When you sell price, you cut profits! Without profits you can't afford to hire qualified people, offer skills development training, provide an ongoing customer satisfaction program, or stay in business long enough to honor the warranty.

- **Future profits are undermined**–Low prices lock you into a vicious cycle of low prices! When a customer brags to a friend about the low price they got from you, you may get a call from the friend . . . but be assured the friend will expect the same low price your customer received.

- **You work twice as hard for the same money**–If you want to keep the same profits you'd make with a 40% gross margin and cut your price 10%, you must increase sales by 1/3. If you cut your price 20%, you have to double the number of sales. A 30% discount requires a 400% increase in sales.

- **Buyer's expectations are lowered**–Price is visual evidence of value! When properly informed, customers use price as a clue about your equipment and installation. A high price can indicate concern for the customer's welfare and increase their expectations. Low prices create fear, uncertainty and doubt.

- **No differentiation**—When products appear equal, people buy the lowest price! But when given a choice, most people will pay more for your customized solution if it provides wanted benefits no one else offers. Being different and better is your greatest advantage; don't lose it. When you're selling price, you're selling a commodity, and the lowest-priced commodity always wins.

- **Customers may never be satisfied**—The customer only has to pay once to be extremely satisfied, but the high cost of a low price goes on forever.

- **You buy expensive customers**—When you sell price, you get price buyers! One of the price buyer's greatest joys in life is grinding you down. Many of these folks specialize in performing "profit-ectomies" on unwary price sellers. You know the drill. The phone calls playing you against your competition, the request for multiple sales calls and free consulting, then the plea for a sharper pencil. Before you know it, you've got hours invested in a job with no profits.

- **You're acquiring unneeded stress**—When you sell price, you buy stress! Many price-buyers are irrationally demanding, want something for nothing and can be a great source of long-term misery. Who needs it?

- **You get disloyal customers**—People that always buy the lowest price are always disloyal! The next time they have a need, they'll buy from whomever has the lowest price. It is impossible to always have the lowest price, because there is always some *fool* willing to sell what you're selling for $50 less.

· **Good customers may be driven off**—It is virtually impossible to satisfy price-only buyers! Minor problems are always major issues that they'll use to squeeze you some more. These folks take so much of your time complaining and asking for concessions, you don't have time to take care of your good customers. Simple neglect is the number one reason customers are lost.

· **You eliminate the price floor**—If you cut your price once, people expect you'll cut it again...and again...and again.

· **You lose trust and credibility**—When you lose trust, you lose everything! A $300 price cut may send a message to the customer that you were overcharging them by $300 in the first place.

· **You may not get paid**—Look at your records: the slow-pays and no-pays are almost always price-only buyers. If you're going to work for free, why not go fishing instead?

· **You get really busy**—The goal of business is not creating work; it is creating profits. Firms that sell price are the busiest the day before they go bankrupt.

More than 80% of Boomers will pay more for additional benefits, faster results and superior solutions to their problems. When all the facts are in, neither you nor your customers can afford the high cost of a low price.

EIGHT

Pre-sold Boomer referrals are the
foundation of financial freedom.

Focus on Referrals

The key to Boomer Selling is implementation. Of course, the problem with implementing any new multi-step process is that pesky hunk of gray matter between our ears that only lets us think one thought at a time. When you try to focus on each individual step in the process, it's easy to lose sight of the whole and end up tripping over yourself. Just visualize your first day on the golf course or ski slope. You can imagine hitting the ball straight down the fairway 300 yards or shushing down a double-black diamond run with refrigerator sized moguls like you're Jean-Claude Killy.

Unfortunately, as you're getting ready to make your first parallel turn on the bunny hill, you start thinking about each step in sequence, running over all the things you've got to do: bend forward slightly; gently plant your pole; lean into the turn with the downhill ski; center your weight over the ball of your downhill foot; apply pressure to the front of your downhill boot; after carving the turn, un-weight your downhill ski...and PHOOSH! There was so much information to process that you lost concentration, crossed your ski tips and did a world-class face plant. On the golf course, you're thinking about keeping your eye on the ball, swinging through the ball, keeping your head down, rotating through the hips, and whipping your wrists through your follow-through, so you take a mighty Tiger Woods-esque cut…and the ball trickles about 20 yards off to the right and spooks a pigeon while your buddies laugh themselves into incontinence.

Every sport has one key element we put our focus on when things start going wrong. In golf the focal point is "Keep your eye on the ball", while with skiing, it's "Keep both hands forward." The point is, you want to internalize the entire process that makes the sport possible so you're doing all the steps automatically, without conscious thought. That's why repetition and practice are everything. Thinking too much can mess you up. Mickey Mantle, the great 1950s center fielder of the New York Yankees, said once when he was sitting next to Ted Williams at an All-Star Game, Williams, one of the greatest students of hitting to ever play the game, started asking Mantle what he did when he hit? Did he pull one hand through first? Which one? When did he shift his weight? And so on. Mantle, always an instinctive ballplayer who relied on his incredible natural talent, went into a terrible slump after that conversation. Why? He was thinking too much at the plate.

— Boomer Selling Insight —
The focal point of Boomer Selling is the referral

Selling is no different. If you try to think about every step in the Boomer Sales process, it's impossible to give your full attention to the buyers and you're very likely to do your best soulless machine impression and lose the sale. To help you get a strong sense of the holistic picture, allow me to focus your attention on the one core goal of Boomer Selling: The referral. That's it. The referral is everything. It's the big red light over the goal that indicates whether or not you've done your job right. Now, that may seem like putting the cart before the horse, but let me explain why it's not. Yes, your focus while you are working with the Boomer customer must be on creating confidence, communicating value and overcoming objections to attain agreement. But the way you'll know that you've done these things well is that you'll get lots of repeat and referral business. If you build the type of rapport and problem-solving skill that wins referrals, you'll automatically be delivering the kind of world-class consultative service that makes your Boomer buyers incredibly loyal, profitable and easy to work with.

When your concentration is on getting the referral instead of getting the order, your subconscious mind automatically adjusts your attitude, behavior and actions from *making* the sale to *satisfying* your customers. When you're selling, you come across as a salesperson; that's just the way it is. But when you're working to satisfy each buyer's wants, needs and desires, you come across as a caring person we'd love to tell our friends about. See the difference? Focusing on referrals not only makes the sales process more fun and less stressful, it makes getting Boomer referrals a whole lot easier. It's like keeping your head down and swinging through the ball on the tee: if you just do those things, you're going to hit the ball soundly every time. The rest is just practice.

> **The goal of Boomer Selling is to create sufficient confidence and value that you will get the referral**

Boomer Selling is Referral Creation

The bottom line is, when satisfied Boomer buyers feel indulged, pampered and fortunate to do business with you, we reward you with referrals. The thing is, if you take great care of us, we want to tell others because they can then see what smart shoppers we are. We were savvy enough to ferret you out—goodness, we must be brilliant! Making us and you look good is a win-win, so give us the chance to do it.

There was a shampoo commercial from the 1970s that illustrates the power of referrals perfectly. It would have been unmemorable except for the phrase, "And they told two friends, and they told two friends, and so on, and so on…" It's one of those bits of cultural trivia that sticks with us. But the most successful businesses in the world have been built this way, by building an army of evangelists who tell friends, who tell friends, who tell more friends. Before you know it you have all the pre-sold referral business you can handle.

We Love Getting Referrals

"I get by with a little help from my friends…"
– The Beatles

Boomers love to get referrals for three very important reasons:

1. They filter noise
2. They save us time
3. They reduce our risk

1. Filter noise. Referrals are the only marketing method that allows us to ask questions and get instant two-way feedback. Boomers are bombarded by thousands of advertising messages per day and, quite frankly, we're sick of it. After lifesaving drugs and the Internet, we're convinced that the greatest invention of our age is Tivo, because it allows us to record *Law and Order* while fast-forwarding past all those commercials that tell us to tell our doctors what drugs we should be taking. We also love referrals because:

- Referrals are more objective than advertising, and the more objective the message, the more we're likely to believe it and act on it

- Because Boomers prefer buying what has already been accepted by others, referrals are more powerful than any advertising

- Boomers are at least six times more likely to believe the opinions of their peers than any form of advertising

- We know our friends have nothing to gain from giving us referrals (in fact, as I said before, there is some risk involved), so their referrals provide more credibility than all other forms of lead generation combined

2. Save time. Many old-school car sale managers have a saying: "Time equals commitment." The theory goes, the more time they could get you to "invest" in the sales process with their silly tricks and lame stalling tactics, the less likely you would be to go through the same painful and time consuming experience with another car dealer.

In other words, they would wear you down with lots of "I have to talk to my sales manager" nonsense. Way to build trust and loyalty, geniuses.

That *so* does not work with Boomers. A major purchase usually takes longer to buy, and we know this going in. But we Boomers have learned that if we want to reduce the amount of time we spend looking for a remodeling contractor, a boat or an attorney, the first thing we get before we go shopping is a good referral. When we go to the right resource the first time, we not only save hours or days of our precious and dwindling time, we reduce our stress level and, as a result, might even live a couple of minutes longer.

3. Reduce risk. Seventy percent of Americans rely on the advice of others when selecting a new doctor. The numbers for selecting lawyers and contractors aren't far below that. Why? Because we're not willing to risk our health, rights or home giving some novice on-the-job-training. Boomers value certainty over uncertainty. We learned long ago (sometime around the Lyndon B. Johnson administration) that the best way to avoid problems and get what we want the first time is by talking to someone who already owns what we're thinking of buying. They've spent all the time and done the research and we get to turn in their homework without the least bit of guilt. How cool is that?

That's called *leveraging our communal knowledge base.* That means, we're finding other people like us who have similar values and desires and finding out who gave them the best experience. That someone should be you. And there are ways to ensure that it is you.

We're Not Natural Referrers

To say Boomer buying behavior is complex is a gross understatement. We are, hands down, the most complicated people with whom you will ever work—smart and insecure, vain and direct, confident and suspicious. And boy-oh-boy, do we know the value of every penny. If you hone your skills successfully selling to Boomers, you can make a great living selling to anyone. We're the original "tough room."

Here's another tricky contradiction about us: Boomers will go out of our way to get referrals from our friends and neighbors before making a major purchase, but will hesitate to give these same folks a referral. The reason is that no matter how sure we are about the service provider we're referring them to, we're afraid our referral could create unrealistic expectations we'd have to hear about or deal with. We dread the Saturday morning phone call saying, "Janet, this is Sally. I went to that chiropractor you recommended and I have to tell you, I've never been in so much pain in all my life." We'll do anything to avoid dropping that kind of stink bomb into our social circle and making ourselves look dumb to boot.

The trouble is that if we like you, we tend to gush. You know how this works: you ask a friend if they've seen any good movies lately, their eyes light up and they start raving about the storyline, superb acting and awarding winning cinematography. You can't wait to buy a ticket and a big bucket of overpriced popcorn. But, by the time you see this overhyped movie your expectations are so high that no matter how good it is you're somehow disappointed. Instead of *Dr. Zhivago*, you get *Heaven's Gate*. You got set up by false expectations, and the simple truth is that tastes are personal (you may have loved *Heaven's Gate*.) One person's treasure is another's trash.

Referrals are a two-edged sword. We love to share our feelings, thoughts and opinions with just about anyone who will seriously listen, but we've all gotten a phone call or a jab in the ribs at the water cooler from a friend or associate who had a bad experience from someone we referred. Unless we're almost positive our friends will get the same level of satisfaction we received, we're not going to refer you. We refuse to be on the hook for your bad performance. You've got to make our approval of you 98% bulletproof before we'll take the risk of referring you. That's what the Boomer Selling process is all about.

Making Referrals Inevitable

Ordinary salespeople think the sale ends when the customer buys. Foolish mortals. You're not a salesperson, you're…Consultant Man or Woman! Faster than a speeding discount! Able to change the course of mighty objections! Able to leap tall display racks in a single bound! Forward-thinking, highly paid consultants see the end of the sale as the beginning of an amazing opportunity to fill their pipeline with pre-sold future sales. They know the end of the sale marks the start of Referral Season. Just as members of the House of Representatives are always campaigning, you should always be focusing on referrals.

Here are the keys to creating an endless flow of high-affinity referral prospects that will make you incredible commissions:

1. Exceed Expectations—It is impossible to get ongoing referrals by providing bottom-tier solutions and "me too" service. If you don't stand out as a provider of value, there's no reason for Boomers to refer you, because Boomers can find low prices anywhere. The number one reason Boomers will give you a referral is that you exceeded our expectations. That's not an easy task with the skeptical, demanding, "Been there, done that," generation, and it's almost impossible when you're selling bottom-benefit products and low-end solutions. Customers who buy entry-level products usually expect much more than they get. These customers are almost certain to have complaints that their minimum cost purchase will never resolve, no matter how much time and effort you invest. When they discover they're stuck with what they bought, who do you think they're going to blame when they talk to their friends?

This is the reason you should always focus on selling quality, performance and value and let price take care of itself. Boomers who purchase the products and accessories that do the best job of solving their problems—making price a secondary issue as long as their perceived value is sky-high—are always the most satisfied.

Not to put too fine a point on it, the more we can brag about what we've bought from you, the more referrals you will get. Boomers who buy the best are much more inclined to tell others. The

> **The only way to consistently exceed Boomers' expectations is with premium, customized solutions**

more extraordinary the solution, the more we'll go out of our way to talk about it. We want to look smart, wise, sophisticated and tasteful. Because every customized solution is tailored to meet each buyer's individual needs, it is always rare and costly. Scarcity and uniqueness are two of the most overlooked reasons Boomers gladly join your secret sales force. We love to feel that we're like no one else.

There's also the phenomenon of not just keeping up with the Joneses, but of kicking the living daylights out of them in the Consumer Olympics medal count. Back during the Cold War, if the USSR added two nuclear missiles, the USA added four. This caused the Soviets to add eight, forcing the US to add 16, and so on (just like the shampoo commercial!). Maybe this is where Boomers got the idea that the next whatever we buy has to be better than what our friends have. We don't want to be looked at with scorn or pity when we violate the social code and—gasp!—downsize to a simpler car or a smaller McMansion. When potential customers are referred by Boomers, it's very likely they'll buy something better than their friends bought—sometimes, *much* better.

— *Boomer Selling Insight* —
When deployed correctly, Boomer Selling can provide all the pre-sold premium buyers you'll ever need

2. **Follow up after the sale**—One of the few positive things that came out of the Carter administration was a study into consumer buying behavior by a group named the Technical Assistance Research Project (TARP.) One of the most important things the survey found was for every complaint received, the average company has 26 customers with problems the seller doesn't know about, of which six could be described as serious. From what you know about Boomers, what do you think the chances are we'll give you a good referral if we have an unresolved

problem? The correct answer is slim to none, and Slim just bought a bus ticket out of town.

It gets worse. Instead to telling you about minor problems, dissatisfied buyers will tell their unhappy story at least nine times. Thirteen percent of your disgruntled former customers will tell more than 20 people why they're ticked off with you, your company or your product. We're far more likely to talk about negative experiences than positive ones, that's just Boomer nature. With enough unresolved problems it doesn't take long to poison your entire pool of potential buyers.

Here's the good news: customers who have a problem that is immediately resolved to their satisfaction will be *more* loyal and *more* likely to do business with you again than those that didn't have problems in the first place. On average, these "made-happy" customers will refer five people by telling about the fair treatment they received from you. The key to future referrals is to find and fix the source of concern *immediately!*

As Bill Clinton and Richard Nixon learned to their chagrin, the cover-up hurts infinitely more than

> **Like the bumper sticker says, "Stuff happens"**

the crime. Don't try to wish customer service challenges away, stall or point fingers. Own up to the problem and treat it as an opportunity to prove your commitment to customer satisfaction. After the sale, send a thank you note and call within 24 hours. Ask your newest customers if they have any questions, need more information or have any concerns you can immediately address. Remember, there's never a traffic jam on the extra mile.

3. Ask for testimonials—In a court of law the most compelling evidence is always first-person testimony, someone saying, "I was there and I saw it happen." After the buyer has a chance to really get involved with their new customized solution (usually about a week or so), call once again and ask, "Is everything still going okay?" If for some reason they're not 100% satisfied, do whatever you must to make them happy. When they answer, "Yes", ask, "Would you mind telling me exactly what you're happy with?" They'll usually tell you three or four things. Next, ask them, "Would you do me a favor? Would you mind writing me a short note outlining what you just said? I'd love to share your comments with my clients." Some Boomers will actually take the time to write you a testimonial note or e-mail. The ones who don't have just reviewed three or four exciting things to tell their friends.

4. Keep in contact—Loyalty is always conditional. You are always in the process of building layer after layer of confidence with your long-term customers and the people they refer. Unfortunately, that layer is like expensive slate tile, which takes thousands of years to build up in the earth, one sedimentary level on top of another, but can be cracked and broken with the tap of a hammer. Loyalty always demands that you continue providing the same level of value and service, again and again. Fall short once and you can set your relationships back years.

A study commissioned by a Canadian service contracting association revealed the value of staying in touch with customers. The study showed most service contractors only get a small fraction of available repeat business. Ninety percent of respondents were satisfied with the work the contractor did, but when asked, "How did you find the contractor?" only 15% said they had used the contractor previously. It's hard to get referrals from folks who forgot with whom they did business with.

— Boomer Selling Insight —
The time you invest staying in touch with
premium Boomer buyers is the most productive,
least expensive marketing you'll ever do

We really don't want to feel like Glenn Close's character in *Fatal Attraction*: "I'm not going to be *ignored!*" To keep us from feeling like a cheap one-night stand, continue to show you care and treat us as someone special. Make a habit of reading the newspaper and magazines, and when you come across something that relates to a customer who bought one of your premium pack-ages—perhaps a hobby or special interest—e-mail it or clip it and send it. We'll be tickled that you took the time and we'll think about how we can return the favor.

The best way we know how to thank you is with re-ferrals. Boomers practice the law of reciprocity: when someone goes out of their way to do something special for us, we feel obligated to return like behavior. That's the way our parents raised us. We know that in a world where so many companies and service providers are just out to make a buck and don't give a flip about their cus-tomers, those who actually care are worth their weight in gold.

5. Make it Easy to Refer You

"I read somewhere that everybody on this planet is separated from everyone else by only six other people."
—*John Guare, Six Degrees of Separation*

Everybody knows 10 people who know 10 people who know 10 people.

Ten satisfied Boomers have the potential to refer 1,000 buyers. Empires have been built that way. But to take advantage of this exponential business opportunity, you *must* make it easy for Boomers to refer you!

Don't be shy; Boomers know referrals are the corner-stone of smart business. We also know you want us to refer people, and if you've met or exceeded our expectations we probably will.

— Boomer Selling Insight —
Make it easy for us to give you referrals

One of the least expensive and most overlooked referral tools is the simple business card. People are much more likely to call you based on a business card given to them by a friend or acquaintance than the most expensive advertising you can do. Look at your business card and ask yourself, if you didn't know anything about this company and received this card, what would motivate you to call? If you're not happy with your answer, or all your latest contact information isn't included, get new cards. At every *appropriate* opportunity, always give two cards to everyone, saying, "Here's one for your file and one to pass along to anyone you feel I can help." Don't forget to also include two business cards in all customer correspondence. It's like chicken soup: it can't hurt.

For goodness sake, have a decent website. Your website is your resume. Even though the people that Boomers refer might be interested in you, they're extremely likely to go to your firm's website before contacting you, so they can check you out in advance without any sales pressure. That's the main reason sales-averse people go to websites. A vast percentage of referral customers will silently "interview" you in the comfort and anonymity of cyberspace. If your website isn't professional and easy to navigate, or doesn't provide at least the basic information they seek, they will probably contact someone else whose site was designed since 1994.

6. Follow up on every referral—Finally, when we give you a referral, tell us the outcome (good, bad or ugly) as soon as possible. Bad news isn't like wine; it doesn't get better with age. If we hear about a negative experience from you before we hear it from the person we referred, our referral pipeline is still going to be open, as long as your conduct was honorable and you did the best you could for the people we referred, even if you couldn't solve their problem. But if we don't hear bad news from you first, kiss any future referrals goodbye.

When you follow-up on referrals, you show that you care enough to spend the time to find out what happened and to keep us informed. Most important, you've proven once again why we placed our confidence in you in the first place.

The Boomer Selling process ends with referral creation. Focus on being the type of consultative sales resource who gets eager referrals and the rest will take care of itself. If you're getting all the referrals that you can handle and a consistent flow of delighted Boomer customers returning to you for more premium products and services, you'll know you've mastered Boomer Selling.

Now, before we go our separate ways, a quick review of the steps of the process:

1. Create Confidence—When you nurture an exceptional level of confidence in us about you, your company and your solution, we not only remember you, we'll go out of our way to refer you and the products you recommend. We want to trust you, but you've got to give us a reason to. Once we do, all the other steps in the process become very easy and extremely natural.

— Boomer Selling Insight —
Our confidence in you is the
foundation of all future referrals

2. Determine Desires—The key to getting referrals is exceeding each Boomer buyer's expectations. To do this, you must determine our desires. What do we want? What do we fear? What deep emotional motivations do we have for buying? Once you know our wants, needs and desires, it's easy for you to promise us a lot and deliver even more.

3. Customize Solutions—Satisfied buyers provide the most abundant referrals. The most satisfied buyers are

Boomers who purchase products and services that do the best job of solving our unique problems. We have a strong drive to feel that our challenges are unusual and unlike those of anyone else. That means you've got to treat us as unique individuals and offer tailored ways to meet our needs. Your one-of-a-kind, premium, customized solution is the foundation of our satisfaction.

4. Reduce Risk—Boomers will give you referrals if we believe you offer the lowest physical, psychological, functional, financial and social risk. If, after dealing with you we feel that:

- Our physical security and emotional comfort are satisfied
- That we're savvy consumers
- That what you've sold us will deliver as promised
- That we've gotten the best value for our money
- That others will admire us for the other four...

...then you're going to get our referral.

5. Elevate Emotions—We are all about emotions. Whether we want to admit it or not, our buying decisions are driven largely by emotions, especially feelings that link us to times in our past that have powerful meaning.

It's your job to discover the emotions that are driving us and to stoke those emotions with insightful questions and keen observations.

6. Validate Value—When you validate the value that you're offering for the price, you not only give Boomers the information we need to justify buying, you also provide memorable facts we can use to share with our friends when talking about you and your customized solution. Remember, value trumps price. If you give us multiple points of value, we will love your solution so much we'll tell everyone.

7. Attain Agreement—Close the sale *not* by applying a high-pressure tactic but by closing the gap between the solution you know you can provide and what the Boomer buyer knows we truly desire. By highlighting value and providing a detailed description of what makes your solution unique, you'll disarm our objections and counter our need to comparison shop, because you will become the only one who can provide what you can provide. When both parties agree that's the case, the sale is finished.

And finally, focus on the referral. Boomers will never refer anyone if we feel they'll be tricked or manipulated into buying. Our referrals reflect upon us, which is why it's so vital that you treat referrals like gold. If we think for a second that the people we refer will experience sales pressure or have their objections dismissed with the wave of a hand, we'll drop you like Buster Douglas dropped Mike Tyson. With Boomer Selling, instead of making us feel pressured, you make buying the natural conclusion and working out the final details amazingly easy.

We Boomers are tough shoppers; we're not easy to please. You must sell the way we want to buy, but it can be done, and when you can do it, you'll never have more lucrative or more appreciative customers. We can be the cornerstone of your career and your income. Come and get us.

INDEX